First World War
and Army of Occupation
War Diary
France, Belgium and Germany

1 INDIAN CAVALRY DIVISION
Lucknow Cavalry Brigade
Headquarters
11 August 1914 - 31 December 1916

WO95/1174/1

The Naval & Military Press Ltd
www.nmarchive.com
Published in association with The National Archives

Published by

The Naval & Military Press Ltd

Unit 10 Ridgewood Industrial Park,

Uckfield, East Sussex,

TN22 5QE England

Tel: +44 (0) 1825 749494

www.naval-military-press.com

www.nmarchive.com

This diary has been reprinted in facsimile from the original. Any imperfections are inevitably reproduced and the quality may fall short of modern type and cartographic standards.

© Crown Copyright
Images reproduced by permission of The National Archives, London, England, 2015.

Contents

Document type	Place/Title	Date From	Date To
Heading	WO95/1174/1		
Heading	B.E.F. France & Flanders 1 Indian Cavalry Div Lucknow Brigade. H.Q. 1914 Aug To 1916 Dec. 1 Kings Dragoon Guards 1914 Aug To 1916 Dec. 29 Lancers. 1914 Aug To 1916 Dec. 36 Jacobs Horse. 1914 Aug To 1916 Dec.		
Heading	War Diary of Hdqrs Lucknow Cavalry Brigade From 11-8-14 To 31-12-14 Volume I		
War Diary	Simla	11/08/1914	07/09/1914
War Diary	Lucknow	10/09/1914	10/09/1914
War Diary	Allahabad	09/09/1914	09/09/1914
War Diary	Simla	09/09/1914	16/09/1914
War Diary	Lucknow	21/09/1914	22/09/1914
War Diary	Simla	25/09/1914	25/09/1914
War Diary	Bombay	10/10/1914	12/10/1914
War Diary	Simla	12/10/1914	12/10/1914
War Diary	Bombay	15/10/1914	16/10/1914
War Diary	Maracilles	07/11/1914	07/11/1914
War Diary	Orleans	23/11/1914	07/12/1914
War Diary	Lillers	09/12/1914	22/12/1914
War Diary	Norrent Fontes	23/12/1914	23/12/1914
War Diary	Heuchin	25/12/1914	08/01/1915
War Diary	Festubert	09/01/1915	11/01/1915
War Diary	Heuchin	12/01/1915	31/01/1915
Miscellaneous	Appendices 1-4		
Miscellaneous	A Form. Messages And Signals.		
Heading	War Diary of Lucknow Cavalry Brigade. From 1st February 1915 to, 28th February 1915		
War Diary	Heuchin	01/02/1915	28/02/1915
Heading	War Diary with Appendices of Lucknow Cavalry Brigade. From 1st March 1915 To 31st March 1915		
War Diary	Heuchin	01/03/1915	04/03/1915
War Diary	Febvin	07/03/1915	10/03/1915
War Diary	Bois Des Dames	11/03/1915	11/03/1915
War Diary	Auchel	12/03/1915	14/03/1915
War Diary	Febvin	15/03/1915	15/03/1915
War Diary	Ligny-Lez-Aire	16/03/1915	16/03/1915
War Diary	Ligny	17/03/1915	17/03/1915
War Diary	Liettres	18/03/1915	31/03/1915
Operation(al) Order(s)	Operation Order No 1 by Major General H.D. Fanshawe, C.B., Commanding 1st Indian Cavalry Division. App 1	10/03/1915	10/03/1915
Operation(al) Order(s)	Operation Order 1 by Br. Genl. W.H. Fasken Comdg Lucknow Cavy Bde App 2	10/03/1915	10/03/1915
Miscellaneous	A Form. Messages And Signals.		
Miscellaneous	II		
Miscellaneous	A Form. Messages And Signals.		
Miscellaneous	A Form. Messages And Signals. App 3		
Miscellaneous	A Form. Messages And Signals. App 4		
Miscellaneous	A Form. Messages And Signals. App 5		

Type	Description	Start	End
Operation(al) Order(s)	Operation Order No. 2 by Major General H.D. Fanshawe, C.B., Commanding 1st Indian Cavalry Division. App 6	14/03/1915	14/03/1915
Miscellaneous	A Form. Messages And Signals. App 7		
Operation(al) Order(s)	Operation Order No. 2 by Br Genl W.H. Fasken Comdg Lucknow Cavy Bde. App 8	14/03/1915	14/03/1915
Heading	War Diary of Lucknow Cavalry Brigade From 1st April 30th April 1915		
War Diary	Liettres	01/04/1915	24/04/1915
War Diary	1/2 Mile West of St Marie Cappel	25/04/1915	27/04/1915
War Diary	St Jans Ter Biezen	28/04/1915	30/04/1915
Operation(al) Order(s)	1st Indian Cavalry Division Order No. 3. App 1		
Operation(al) Order(s)	Operation Order No 1 by Brig Gen Fasken Comg L.C.B. App 2	24/04/1915	24/04/1915
Miscellaneous	A Form. Messages And Signals.		
Miscellaneous	Messages And Signals.		
Heading	War Diary with Appendices of Lucknow Cavalry Brigade Hd. Qrs from 1st May To 31st May		
War Diary	St Jan Ter Biezen	01/05/1915	01/05/1915
War Diary	1/2 Mile West of Ste Marie Cappel	02/05/1915	04/05/1915
War Diary	Mametz	05/05/1915	16/05/1915
War Diary	Le Reveillon	17/05/1915	17/05/1915
War Diary	Burbure	18/05/1915	18/05/1915
War Diary	Mametz	19/05/1915	26/05/1915
War Diary	Queve D'Oxelaere	27/05/1915	27/05/1915
War Diary	Vlamertinghe	28/05/1915	28/05/1915
Miscellaneous	A Form. Messages And Signals. App 1		
Miscellaneous	A Form. Messages And Signals. App 2		
Miscellaneous	A Form. Messages And Signals.		
Operation(al) Order(s)	1st Indian Cavalry Division Order No. 4. App 3	04/05/1915	04/05/1915
Operation(al) Order(s)	Operation Order No. 2 by Br. Genl W.H Fasken Comdg Lucknow Cavy Bde App 4	04/05/1915	04/05/1915
Miscellaneous	A Form. Messages And Signals.		
Operation(al) Order(s)	1st Indian Cavalry Division Order No. 5. App 5	17/05/1915	17/05/1915
Miscellaneous	A Form. Messages And Signals.		
Operation(al) Order(s)	1st Indian Cavalry Division Order No. 6. App 7	19/05/1915	19/05/1915
Miscellaneous	A Form. Messages And Signals.		
Operation(al) Order(s)	1st Indian Cavalry Divisional Order No. 7. App 9	26/05/1915	26/05/1915
Operation(al) Order(s)	Operation Order No. 3 by Brig-Genl W.H. Fasken, Comdg Lucknow Cav. Bde. App 10	26/05/1915	26/05/1915
Operation(al) Order(s)	1st Indian Cavalry Divisional Order No. 8. App 11	27/05/1915	27/05/1915
Operation(al) Order(s)	Operation Order No. 4 by Brig-Genl W.H. Fasken, Comdg Lucknow Cav. Bde App 12	27/05/1915	27/05/1915
Miscellaneous	A Form. Messages And Signals.		
Miscellaneous	B.M. 452. App 13	28/05/1919	28/05/1919
Miscellaneous	A Form. Messages And Signals.		
Heading	War Diary of Lucknow Cavalry Brigade. From 1st June 1915 To 30th June. 1915		
War Diary	Vlamertinghe	01/06/1915	02/06/1915
War Diary	East of Ypres	03/06/1915	03/06/1915
War Diary	Yeomanry Post & G.H.Q Line Trenches	04/06/1915	05/06/1915
War Diary	Vlamertinghe	06/06/1915	13/06/1915
War Diary	L'Erkels Brugge	14/06/1915	14/06/1915
War Diary	Mametz	15/06/1915	30/06/1915
Heading	War Diary of Lucknow Cavalry Brigade From 1st July 1915 To 31st July 1915		

War Diary	Mametz	01/07/1915	31/07/1915
Heading	War Diary with Appendices of Lucknow Cavalry Brigade From 1st August 1915 To 12th September 1915		
War Diary		01/08/1915	01/08/1915
War Diary	Fruges	02/08/1915	02/08/1915
War Diary	Maresquel	03/08/1915	03/08/1915
War Diary	Houdencourt	04/08/1915	04/08/1915
War Diary	Bertheaucourt	07/08/1915	07/08/1915
War Diary	Canaples	22/08/1915	22/08/1915
War Diary	Forceville	23/08/1915	23/08/1915
War Diary	Authville	24/08/1915	24/08/1915
War Diary	Canaples	28/08/1915	28/08/1915
War Diary	Authville	02/09/1915	02/09/1915
War Diary	Beaucourt	03/09/1915	06/09/1915
War Diary	Authville	12/09/1915	12/09/1915
Operation(al) Order(s)	1st Indian Cavalry Divisional Operation Order No. 12.	20/08/1915	20/08/1915
Operation(al) Order(s)	Operation Order No. 7 by Brig-General W.H. Fasken, Comdg Lucknow Cav Bde.	20/08/1915	20/08/1915
Operation(al) Order(s)	1st Indian Cavalry Division Operation Order No. 14.	31/08/1915	31/08/1915
Operation(al) Order(s)	Operation Order No. 8 by Brig-General W.H. Fasken, Commanding Lucknow Cavalry Brigade.	01/09/1915	01/09/1915
Miscellaneous	Instructions For Led Horse Party		
Miscellaneous	Copy of Administrative Instructions No. Q-3307 dated 1st September 1915. from 1st Indian Cavalry Division.		
Miscellaneous	Movement Table For Led Horse Party 1st Ind. Cav. Divn.		
Heading	War Diary with Appendices of Lucknow Cavalry Brigade From 13th September 1915 To 31st October 1915		
War Diary	Authville	14/09/1915	16/09/1915
War Diary	Beaucourt	17/09/1915	17/09/1915
War Diary	St Leger	21/09/1915	22/09/1915
War Diary	Mon Plaisir	25/09/1915	22/10/1915
War Diary	Cavillon	31/10/1915	31/10/1915
Operation(al) Order(s)	Lucknow Cavalry Brigade Operation Order No. 9	10/09/1915	10/09/1915
Operation(al) Order(s)	Instructions To Accompany Divisional Operation Order No. 16.		
Operation(al) Order(s)	Lucknow Brigade Operation Order No. 10.	14/09/1915	14/09/1915
Miscellaneous	Divisional Table of Led Horse Parties		
Miscellaneous	A Form. Messages And Signals.		
Operation(al) Order(s)	1st Indian Cavalry Division Operation Order No. 19.	22/09/1915	22/09/1915
Miscellaneous	The Division will move to new billeting area on October 22nd as under:- Headquarters. 1st Indian Cavalry Division 20th October 1915	20/10/1915	20/10/1915
Miscellaneous	Administrative Instructions in connection with G.A.404.	20/10/1915	20/10/1915
Miscellaneous	To the O.C. U Battery R.H.A. N.D.Gds 29th Lrs 36th J.H. Sig Troop Mob Vety Section. Bde Transport Officer	20/10/1915	20/10/1915
Miscellaneous	To the O.C. U Battery R.H.A. King's Dragoon Guards. 29th Lancers. 36th Jacob's Horse. Signal Troop. Mobile Veterinary Section. Brigade Transport Officer	21/10/1915	21/10/1915
Heading	War Diary of Lucknow Cavalry Brigade From 1st November 1915 To 30 November 1915		
War Diary	Cavillon	07/11/1915	18/11/1915
War Diary	Vieulaine	31/11/1915	31/11/1915

Miscellaneous	Headquarters. 1st Indian Cavalry Division. 17th November 1915.	17/11/1915	17/11/1915
Miscellaneous	To the O.C. U Battery R.H.A. King's Dragoon Guards. 29th Lancers 36th Jacob's Horse. Signal Troop Mobile Vety Section. Bde Supply Officer Bde Transport Officer Copy to 1st Indian Cavalry Division.	17/11/1915	17/11/1915
Heading	War Diary of Headquarters, Lucknow Cavalry Brigade From 1st December 1915 To 31st January 1915		
War Diary	Vieulaine	14/12/1915	16/12/1915
War Diary	Franleu	31/12/1915	31/01/1916
Miscellaneous	Reference Operation Order No. 11 dated 13th December Indian Cavalry Corps 13th December 1915	13/12/1915	13/12/1915
Miscellaneous	Administrative Instructions. Reference Indian Cavalry Corps Administrative Orders, No. Q-3215, dated 13th December 1915.	14/12/1915	14/12/1915
Miscellaneous	Headquarters, 1st Indian Cavalry Division.	14/12/1915	14/12/1915
Miscellaneous	To the O.C. King's Dragoon Guards, 29th Lancers. 36th Jacob's Horse. Signal Troop. Mobile Veterinary Section. Brigade Supply Officer. Brigade Transport Officer.Headquarters Lucknow Cavalry Bde.	15/12/1915	15/12/1915
Heading	War Diary of Headquarters, Lucknow Cavalry Brigade From 1st February 1916 To 30th April 1916		
War Diary	Franleu	05/02/1916	26/03/1916
War Diary	Vaulx	30/03/1916	30/03/1916
Miscellaneous	Reference Para 3 March Orders dated 24-3-16.	25/03/1916	25/03/1916
Miscellaneous	A Form. Messages And Signals.		
Miscellaneous	March Orders by Brig-General W.H. Fasken. C.B., Commanding Lucknow Cavalry Brigade.	24/03/1916	24/03/1916
Operation(al) Order(s)	1st Indian Cavalry Division Operation Order No. 20.	21/03/1916	21/03/1916
Miscellaneous	March Table		
War Diary	Vaulx	09/04/1916	09/04/1916
War Diary	Yvrench	15/04/1916	19/04/1916
War Diary	Vaulx	20/04/1916	30/04/1916
Heading	War Diary of Headquarters, Lucknow Cavalry Brigade From 1st May 1916 To 30th June 1916		
War Diary	Vaulx	01/05/1916	01/05/1916
War Diary	St Riquier	04/05/1916	07/05/1916
War Diary	Vaulx	10/05/1916	10/05/1916
War Diary	Rebreuve	13/05/1916	30/06/1916
Miscellaneous	To Bdes & Units of Divl Troops. Headquarters 1st Indian Cavalry Division, 28th June 1916	28/06/1916	28/06/1916
Miscellaneous	Scale "A" Mobile L.G.S.W.		
Miscellaneous	Table of Distribution of Tools "A" Echelon.		
Miscellaneous	Marching Order (Summer) Scale "A"		
Heading	War Diary of Headquarters, Lucknow Cavalry Brigade From 1st July 1916 To 31st July 1916		
War Diary	Grouches	01/07/1916	02/07/1916
War Diary	Frohen Le Grand	04/07/1916	19/07/1916
War Diary	Villers Brulin	20/07/1916	21/07/1916
War Diary	Aux Rietz	21/07/1916	22/07/1916
War Diary	Neuville St Vaast	22/07/1916	22/07/1916
War Diary	Rollincourt	23/07/1916	23/07/1916
War Diary	Villers Brulin	24/07/1916	24/07/1916
War Diary	Neuville St Vaast	26/07/1916	26/07/1916
War Diary	Rollincourt	26/07/1916	27/07/1916
War Diary	Villers Brulin	30/07/1916	30/07/1916

War Diary	Chelers	31/07/1916	31/07/1916
Miscellaneous	Headquarters 1st Indian Cavalry Division, 18 July 1916.	18/07/1916	18/07/1916
Miscellaneous	Headquarters, Lucknow Cavalry Brigade. 18 July 1916	18/07/1916	18/07/1916
Miscellaneous	Copy of Q-2316 dated 18-7-16 from 1st Ind Cavalry Division. Administrative Instruction Issued in accordance with C-64		
Miscellaneous	A Form. Messages And Signals.		
Miscellaneous	Reference G-45, dated 18/7/16. Headquarters 1st Indian Cavalry Division. 25th July 1916.	25/07/1916	25/07/1916
Miscellaneous			
Miscellaneous	King's Dragoon Guards.		
Miscellaneous	29th Lrs Digging Party.		
Miscellaneous	36th J. Horse Digging Party		
Miscellaneous	Jodhpur Lrs Digging Party.		
Miscellaneous	Headquarters Lucknow Cav Dbe.		
Miscellaneous	Time Table Of Reliefs 29th July, 1916.		
Heading	War Diary of Headquarters, Lucknow Cavalry Brigade From 1st August 1916 To 31st August 1916		
War Diary	Chelers	01/08/1916	09/08/1916
War Diary	Pas	10/08/1916	31/08/1916
Miscellaneous	A Form. Messages And Signals.		
Operation(al) Order(s)	56th Divisional Order No. 21	07/08/1916	07/08/1916
Miscellaneous	Table "A" Issued with 56th Divisional Order No. 21.		
Miscellaneous	Table "B" Issued with 56th Divisional Order No. 21.		
Operation(al) Order(s)	56th Divisional Order No. 22.	10/08/1916	10/08/1916
Miscellaneous	A Form. Messages And Signals.		
Miscellaneous	137th Inf. Brigade. 138th Inf. Brigade. 139th Inf. Brigade. Lucknow Cav. Brigade. 1/Monmouths. O.C. "P" Coy. Special Bde. R.E. 46th Division 1878/G.	09/08/1916	09/08/1916
Miscellaneous	Carrying Operations, Night of 11th/12th Appendix. A.		
Miscellaneous	Carrying Operations, Night of 12th/13th		
Miscellaneous	Carrying Operations, Night of 13th/14th Amendment to Appx A		
Miscellaneous	Carrying Operations, Night of 13th/14th		
Miscellaneous	With reference to this Office 1878/G of 9th August, 1916, Appendix "A". Owing to altered capacity of emplacements the following amendments are made:-	11/08/1916	11/08/1916
Heading	War Diary of Headquarters Lucknow Cavalry Brigade From 1st September 1916 To 30th September 1916		
War Diary	Pas	01/09/1916	03/09/1916
War Diary	Occoches	04/09/1916	04/09/1916
War Diary	Brailly	11/09/1916	15/09/1916
War Diary	Dernacourt	15/09/1916	20/09/1916
War Diary	Morlancourt	25/09/1916	26/09/1916
War Diary	Montauban	26/09/1916	27/09/1916
War Diary	Bussy Les Daours	28/09/1916	28/09/1916
War Diary	Hangest	29/09/1916	29/09/1916
War Diary	Bois de L'Abbey	30/09/1916	30/09/1916
Operation(al) Order(s)	Lucknow Cavalry Brigade Operation Order No. 1	12/09/1916	12/09/1916
Miscellaneous	March Table to Accompany 1st Indian Cavalry Division Operation Order No. 26.		
Miscellaneous	A Form. Messages And Signals.		
Miscellaneous	Headquarters Lucknow Cavalry Brigade 25th September 1916	25/09/1916	25/09/1916
Miscellaneous	A Form. Messages And Signals.		
Operation(al) Order(s)	1st Indian Cavalry Division Operation Order No. 34	27/09/1916	27/09/1916

Heading	War Diary of Headquarters, Lucknow Cavalry Brigade From 1st October 1916 To 30th November 1916		
War Diary	Crecy	01/10/1916	02/11/1916
War Diary	Moyenneville	17/11/1916	27/11/1916
Heading	War Diary of Headquarters, Lucknow Cavalry Brigade From 1st December 1916 To 31st December 1916		
Heading	War Diary of Lucknow Cavalry Brigade Headquarters. For the month of December, 1916		
War Diary	Moyenneville	01/12/1916	31/12/1916

WO 95/11741

B.E.F. FRANCE & FLANDERS
1 INDIAN CAVALRY DIV
LUCKNOW BRIGADE. H.Q.
1914 AUG TO 1916 DEC.
1 KINGS DRAGOON GUARDS
1914 AUG TO 1916 DEC.
29 LANCERS.
1914 AUG TO 1916 DEC.
36 JACOBS HORSE.
1914 AUG TO 1916 DEC.

B.E.F. FRANCE & FLANDERS.
1 INDIAN CAVALRY DIVISION.
LUCKNOW BRIGADE. H.Q.
 1914 AUG TO 1916 DEC.
 1 KINGS DRAGOON GUARDS
1914 AUG TO 1916 DEC.
 29 LANCERS.
 1914 AUG TO 1916 DEC.
 36 JACOBS HORSE.
 1914 AUG TO 1916 DEC.

War Diary of
Hars Lucknow Cavalry Brigade

From 11 - 8 - 14
To 31 - 12 - 14

Volume I

12/4546
Pp 1 to 9

ORIGINAL

Army Form C. 2118.

WAR DIARY
or
~~INTELLIGENCE SUMMARY.~~
(Erase heading not required.)

Instructions regarding War Diaries and Intelligence Summaries are contained in F. S. Regs., Part II, and the Staff Manual respectively. Title pages will be prepared in manuscript.

8 Cavalry Brigade

Hour, Date, Place.	Summary of Events and Information.	Remarks and references to Appendices.
Simla 11 August	From C.G.S. No. 959/W to G.O.C. 8° Division, detailing orders for the organization of an Expeditionary Force.	To G.O.C. 8° Cav. Bde for information.
Simla 30 August 22 hrs 25 m	From A.G. No 85/7 ordering mobilization of 8° Cavalry Brigade for service with Indian Expeditionary Force A. 17° Cavalry to replace 16° Cavalry. Take over latter's mobilization equipment.	
Simla 1 September	From A.G. no 85 K.G. o.c. 8° Division. The 27° Light Cavalry will supply a squadron of Punjabi mussalmans to replace the Calcutta squadron of the 17° Cavalry; 27° to complete their squadron with field service clothing; All other mobilization equipment to be soldiers of 17°.	
3° September Simla	From M.S. Chief No 1727/4 Appointing Capt. Maitland 14° Lancers Staff Captain of the Brigade	
"	From M.S. Chief No 1727/3 Appointing 2° Lieut Crosse R.F.A. interpreter.	
6 September 16.40 Simla	From Q.S. No 2986/w advising all officers to take 3° chargers	
7 September 18.10 Simla	From Chief G.S. No 3040/W Silaner Cavalry Regiment to take 8 horses in place of their riding camels.	

Army Form C. 2118.

WAR DIARY
or
INTELLIGENCE SUMMARY.   LUCKNOW Cavalry Bde
(Erase heading not required.)

Hour, Date, Place.	Summary of Events and Information.	Remarks and references to Appendices.
10 Sept. Lucknow	From GOC 1st Cavalry Bde to 8th Division – reporting ready except for 8 horses.	
9 Sept. Allahabad	From 17th Cavalry to 8th Cav. Bde reporting that 27 Cav. unable to supply 51 extra horses requires for 10% reserve, signallers & replacing riding camels, no more horses being available except remounts and unfit horses.	
9 Sept. Simla	From MS Chief No 1727/3/10 Asst. Officer to be provided from War Bde – Interpreter additional.	
13 Sept. Simla	From AG No 93/4. A.S.I.A. deficiency in horses 8 17 to be made up from 36. Horses required for B.R. Signal troop to come from War Establishment of Regts.	
13 Sept. Simla	From M.S. Chief No 1727/3 Appointing Major Taylor 19 Lancers Brigade Major vice Captain Tovie detained England.	
14 Sept. Simla	From Gen. Staff Cav. Divn. No 12/1/R Machine guns will be replaced on arrival at destination by machine guns from home firing mark 7 ammunition.	
14 Sept. Simla	From Chief Gen Staff No 3505 W machine gun officers brain with 9th Cav. Bde.	

P.T.O.

Army Form C. 2118.

WAR DIARY
or
INTELLIGENCE SUMMARY.
(Erase heading not required.)

Hour, Date, Place.	Summary of Events and Information.	Remarks and references to Appendices.
16 Sept Simla	From Gen Staff Cav Divn No 12/3/R. Supply of officers for KDG is being considered & requirements will be arranged if possible, though not necessarily before embarkation.	* Delay in mobilisation caused partly by difficulty in collecting transportation necessities and fortnight men
21 Sept Lucknow 22 Sept Lucknow	From O Cav Bde & S.B. Divn. Mobilisation reported complete. * Lieut W. F. Blacker 36 Jacob's Horse appointed Commanding Signal Troop	
25 Sept Simla	From M.S. Chief No 1727/14 to GOC O Divn. Following as Chief orders regarding Officers Indian Cav Bde. KDG. Lt detained England. 17 accompany Regt from India. I remain at depot AAA It has been noted Regt is 5 short of establishment AAA 15 Cavalry 2 officers including Capt Kirkwood detained England. 8 officers only including same from 17 Cavalry should therefore accompany Regt from India balance being left at depot AAA 36 Horse 4 officers detained England. 8 officers only should accompany Regt from India, balance been left at depot AAA	
	The Brigade entrained at peace stations for Bombay between 6" and 10" October. On arrival at Bombay on 9" Oct.	
10 October Bombay	U Battery R.H.A came under the orders of the C.R.A. Cav Bde. 17th Cavalry had a repeated case of plague. P.i.T.	

Army Form C. 2118.

WAR DIARY
or
INTELLIGENCE SUMMARY. LUCKNOW Cavalry Bde

(Erase heading not required.)

Hour, Date, Place.	Summary of Events and Information.	Remarks and references to Appendices.
12' October Bombay	Glanders established in 17' Cavalry	
12' October Simla	From C.G.S. No. 6429 - 29' Lancers will replace 17' Cavalry	
15' October Bombay	29' Lancers completed arrival in Bombay, thus completing the Arrival	
16' October Bombay	8' Cav. Rde. sailed in Cav. Divism. Convoy	
7' November Marseilles	The Brigade began to disembark, but the last unit did not arrive until the 16'. The casualties on the voyage were 1st K.D.G's 9 horses 2q' Lancers 3 — 36' Jacobs Horse 10 — After being in camp or billets for a few days, the units of the Brigade were entrained for Orleans where the last unit of the Brigade (1st K.D.G's) arrived on the 22'. The casualties in Marseilles were 2q' Lancers 1 horse 36' Jacobs Horse 3 —	
23' Nov. Orleans	For the first few days in la Source camp (Orleans) the weather was very wet. From the 16' the weather has been frosty with a N.E. wind, but the horses are picking up + doing well.	Right

Army Form C. 2118.

WAR DIARY
or
INTELLIGENCE SUMMARY.   LUCKNOW Cavalry Bde.
(Erase heading not required.)

Instructions regarding War Diaries and Intelligence Summaries are contained in F.S. Regs., Part II, and the Staff Manual respectively. Title pages will be prepared in manuscript.

Hour, Date, Place.	Summary of Events and Information.	Remarks and references to Appendices.
26th November Orleans	The Brigade should have started entraining for railhead this day, but owing to look up amongst the transport horses, transport could not be issued. Arrangements are being made to provide transport at railhead.	
4th December Orleans	Major General C. Cookson left for MARSEILLES to meet the MEERUT Bde & the New Bde. from India.	
7th December Orleans	The Brigade began entraining for railhead at 20.25 and finished entraining at 18.55 in the 8th.	
9th December LILLERS	H.Q. Staff, 11th K.D.Gs, & 29th Lancers detrained and went into billets H.Q. Staff & 11th K.D.Gs at LILLERS 29th Lancers at HAUT RIEUX V Battery R.H.A. joined the Bde. Colonel D.H. Fasken arrived and assumed command of the Brigade and D.H.A. Fasken arrived and went into billets 2 squadrons & HQ at BAC RIEUX	
10th December LILLERS	36th Lancers detrained and went into billets 2 squadrons & HQ at HAUT RIEUX and packs W at LILLERS. The billets area is very cramped, most of the horses at HAUT RIEUX and BAC RIEUX being in the open	Rue—

Army Form C. 2118.

WAR DIARY
or
INTELLIGENCE SUMMARY.

(Erase heading not required.)

LUCKNOW Cavalry Bde

Hour, Date, Place.	Summary of Events and Information.	Remarks and references to Appendices.
14th December 6:30 am LILLERS	Orders received by Bde ordering to be ready at one hours notice. 1st & 2nd L.H. were packed, water carts filled, and the Brigade stood to.	
15 December LILLERS	The Brigade still ready to move (N) but as men billets spread was available, the 2 squadrons of the 36th Horse at BAC RIEUX went to Lencare vacating to BAC	
19th December LILLERS	Moved to ECQUEDECQUES the 29' Lancers vacating to BAC RIEUX	
22' December LILLERS	The Bde 19th ready to move at short notice.	
23 December MORRENT PONTES	Rode mad at 6 am to area MORRENT PONTES – ST HILAIRE – ROMBLY	
25 December HEUCHIN	36th Horse moved to HAM from ROMBLY	
26 December HEUCHIN	Bde moved to area FIEFS – PREDEFIN – LISBOURG – HEUCHIN	
27th December HEUCHIN	Major TAYLOR learns to take up appointment of E.S.O. 1 Indian Cavalry Division Captain MUSPRATT takes up the appointment of Brigade Major Lucknow Cav. Bde. vice Major TAYLOR.	
31st December HEUCHIN	LIVOSSART also visited is billeting area. No other change	

L Stanford Major 31/12
Brigade Major

Army Form C. 2118.

WAR DIARY
or
INTELLIGENCE SUMMARY.
(Erase heading not required.)

Instructions regarding War Diaries and Intelligence Summaries are contained in F. S. Regs., Part II, and the Staff Manual respectively. Title pages will be prepared in manuscript.

Lucknow Cavly Bde.

ADJUTANT GENERAL INDIA
1118 W.D.
- 7. FEB 1915
BASE OFFICE

Hour, Date, Place.	Summary of Events and Information.	Remarks and references to Appendices.
1st January 1915 HEUCHIN	In billets HEUCHIN area	
8th Jany HEUCHIN	No Change	
9th Jany FESTUBERT	Bde ordered to do 48 hours spell in trenches from evening of 9th relieving SIALKOT Cav Bde. The Bde, consisting of 300 infantry from each Cav. Regt. was transported by motor lorries to BETHUNE and marched from there to FESTUBERT via RUE DE BETHUNE where Bde HQrs remained. The 1 Battalion S. Wales Bord: on general reserve & Bde. section came under the orders of G.O.C. the relief of SIALKOT Cav B.de. was effected between 7.20 p.m. & 2.40 a.m. 10th Jany. Relief was slow owing to the bring very mud particularly bad into the trenches upon the steady & incessant number of relieved troops after many hours in flooded trenches. Some considerable movements to & fro burning stacks which disclosed movements to the enemy.	Refrence MERVILLE - LA BASSEE map 1/40000
10th Jany FESTUBERT	The Position which was part of front held by 7th (British) Division, was held from Right centre in 36°J. Home Centre between 29 & 30 Lancers left sector K.D.G. Right Regt h.ad 2 squadrons in firing line, one in support one in log'... Lineal reserve. Extent of front held about 1½ miles inclusively East of LE PLANTIN and FESTUBERT village	

WAR DIARY or INTELLIGENCE SUMMARY

Army Form C. 2118.

(Erase heading not required.)

Hour, Date, Place.	Summary of Events and Information.	Remarks and references to Appendices.
10th January 1915 Continued	The section on our right were held by 1. Bde. TOT on our left by 6. Bde. Morning passed quietly. Bde firing some bursts of rifle fire in accordance with Div orders & claims. At 1:15 p.m. an arty shell burst in trenches and at 2 p.m. in front of stay point, Pioneer Farm moving it to right. In the triangle south of E.AMS.H.5.8.E canal which was being established by 2 P.M. At 12 noon and 3:30 p.m. messages were received from 1st Div suggesting methods for preventing troops from being detailed in deep water. The General performed was that reports of numbers sent to hospital should be made if snow withdrawn & dry and carried away on this. It was decided to notice night periods subordination by 50 min. Back & after instruction 3.30 min. Orders were given that Div some enemy rifles were cut. 6 p.m. Some casualties were sustained during enemy rifles exploring Stat. If machine gun reports were & would evacuate front place in the position and order new men drop in next place.	Apps. 1 & 2 App. 3
11th Jany. 1915 FESTUBERT	At 1 a.m. O.C. left instruction - here by next - reports under intense, adverse weather - reports E & D. Dr. Shoreds membership. Reports E. I. Dr. showed 2.8.0 & D.com between. After enquiring from 17 Adr. Walker informed most HgF from front Bde & trenches lands after this line, IS - I Div. ordered Bde to withdraw to support trenches about 300 - troops in rear this withdrawal was carried out under cover without incident. All the fire was finally withdrawn by 7 a.m.	App. 4

Army Form C. 2118.

WAR DIARY
or
INTELLIGENCE SUMMARY.
(Erase heading not required.)

[Location:] Lachau... Canton

Hour, Date, Place.	Summary of Events and Information.	Remarks and references to Appendices.

11th Jany cont? — The line run from southern end LE PLANTIN village along eastern edge village, passed just east of southern out-skirts of FESTUBERT then diverged sharply E.N.E. to southern end of south east of brewing. "M. & G." Bde. in front of main line held 8 officers sent to point out east position of our flanks. New line was held by 2 Sqn. 36 Stren. 2pm 29th Lancers 6 troops 8gn; H2.S in firing line, machine gun 3 rifles in three troops in reserve on Company S. Also Bombing-unit were brought up Point of LE PLANTIN to reserve to make good ... necessary of firing in personnel caused by exhaustion. Punishmen... Patrols sent out in ... ... they had not occupied our firing line trenches. No say passed during the day. Officers ... 11:50 am was carried out. A M.G. from 2nd light was left for the relieving Bn. had ... clumps for use at night on 3 different points. M.T.O.N. Cav. Bn. arrived. N relief carried out with out drawing any hostile fire, were expected by 9 p.m. The Bn. marched back to BETHUNE at 12:30 am Bn. billeted were carried back to its billets arriving there about 8 am.

12th Jany HEUCHIN

Army Form C. 2118.

WAR DIARY
or
INTELLIGENCE SUMMARY.
(Erase heading not required.)

Instructions regarding War Diaries and Intelligence Summaries are contained in F. S. Regs., Part II, and the Staff Manual respectively. Title pages will be prepared in manuscript.

Lucknow Cav Bde

Hour, Date, Place.	Summary of Events and Information.	Remarks and references to Appendices.
12 Jany Continued	The casualties for 9th 10th & 11th inst. were 8 Dfdrs. & 6 rank & file 6 wounded 29 Lancers Nov ranks 2 killed, 15 wounded, 1 missing 36 J. horse Lieut R. DS. OWEN JONES wounded Jemadar SHAM SINGH missing believed killed. Other ranks 5 killed, 6 wounded, 6 missing. ① The weather throughout was wet the roads bad and becoming muddy. The exposure of the men in flooded trenches caused great exhaustion & swollen feet. On an average 70 men per regiment were unable to march back with their unit & had to be sent in carts & ambulances. Of these about 30 men had to be sent to BETHUNE about 100 per regt: were temporarily incapacitated by wet & by swollen feet.	① From subsequent information these figures were corrected to 12 wounded and 1 missing
18th Jany. HEUCHIN	The Indian Cavalry Corps was inspected by the Commander in Chief.	S Hanfy Capt Lucknow Cav Bde
29 Jany HEUCHIN 30 " "	Orders received to be ready to move at 2 hours notice. U Battery R.H.A. ordered to leave the Bde and move at once to STRAZEELE near HAZEBROUCK to join the 28th Division. Battery left 11.30 am	
31 Jany "	Still in same billeting area	

Appendices 1 — 4.

Re reduction of number
of men in flood trenches

"A" Form. Army Form C. 2121.

MESSAGES AND SIGNALS.   No. of Message.

Prefix ___ Code ___ m. | Words | Charge | This message is on a/c of: | Recd. at ___ m.
Office of Origin ___ Service Instructions | Sent | | *app* | Date ___
| | At ___ m. | | Service. | From ___
| | To ___ | | | By ___
| | By ___ | | (Signature of "Franking Officer.") |

TO { LUCKNOW Brigade

Sender's Number | Day of Month | In reply to Number | AAA
G569. | 10th | |

The G.O.C. considers that an effort must be made to move the majority of the troops who are now in deep water or mud in the trenches on to drier ground and He does not wish in any way to tie you down as to the manner in which you will hold your line but he authorises you to hold the trenches with snipers where they are too wet to be fully held withdrawing the remainder into drier ground from which they would be able to counter attack should the

From ___
Place ___
Time ___

The above may be forwarded as now corrected. (Z)

Censor. | Signature of Addressor or person authorised to telegraph in his name

*This line should be erased if not required.
3662 M. & Co. Ltd. Wt. W929/549—100,000. 6/14. Forms C2121/10.

"A" Form.   Army Form C. 2121.

MESSAGES AND SIGNALS.

TO: Page Two.

Sender's Number: G.569
Day of Month: 10th

enemy advance. aaa ~~This method necessitates the use of ... to give the troops ... with confidence ...~~

It must be clearly understood that if troops are withdrawn from the first line, a new line must be selected & trenches constructed.

From: 1st DIV.
Time: 11-5 am

E.J. Hoare Nairne
Lt Col.

"A" Form.
MESSAGES AND SIGNALS.
Army Form C. 2121.
No of Message 53

Prefix S Code C m.
Office of Origin and Service Instructions.

This message is on a/c of:
app Service.
(Signature of "Franking Officer.")

Recd. at _____ m.
Date
From
By

TO — Lucknow Bde.

Sender's Number: G.577
Day of Month: 10th
In reply to Number:
AAA

Reference my G.569 of today the G.O.C. after consultation with Genl. BARROW, MHOW Cav. Bde. & Lt. Col. Schreiber C.R.E. 1st Divn thought that better results would be obtained by baling and pumping present trenches than by digging a new line behind which would be difficult work even with men trained and used to digging AAA If the Bde. Commander wished he could reduce the number of men in the trenches to groups of 2 or 3 to 10 yards keeping the remainder behind under cover — active, not asleep, but ready to counter-attack, and within counter-attacking distance AAA Previous to last heavy rain the trenches were fairly dry — so baling and pumping should have good result AAA The G.O.C. would like to know as early as convenient what you have decided to do to hold the position tonight.

From 1st DIVN
Place
Time 2-50 pm

E. Hoare Nairne
Lt. Col. G.S.

The above may be forwarded as now corrected. (Z)
BM 20
Cd 3.35
Censor. Signature of Addressor or person authorised to telegraph in his name
*This line should be erased if not required.

"A" Form. Army Form C. 2121.
MESSAGES AND SIGNALS.

TO: 1st Div

Sender's Number: BM 94
Day of Month: 10
AAA

Have ordered to make only following reductions in firing trenches tonight. Right subsection 50 centre 50 left subsection 31 aaa It may be found possible to make further reductions later

From: Lucknow Cav Bde

Time: 8 45 p

"A" Form.
MESSAGES AND SIGNALS.
Army Form C. 2121.

Prefix	Code	m.	Words	Charge	This message is on a c of:	Recd. at	m.
Office of Origin and Service Instructions.			Sent			Date	
			At ____ m.		Service.	From	4
			To			By	
			By		(Signature of "Franking Officer")		

TO 1st Div

Sender's Number	Day of Month	In reply to Number	AAA
BM 97	11		

Water in trenches in left subsection held by K.D.G's is rising & there is possibility of trenches becoming untenable about from 6.30 am K.D.G — have been ordered to hold their trenches with 30 snipers only and company S.W.B. has been ordered up in local reserve to replace exhausted men of K.D.G. aaa Water difficulty now so great that alternative appears the construction of breastwork behind present trench or evacuation of ground aaa as Division wishes security of ground right and left could matter be discussed with General Staff 1st Div this morning aaa addressed 1st Div repeated 6 Bde

From	Lucknow Cav Bde
Place	
Time	1.15 am

The above may be forwarded as now corrected (Z)

Serial No 777

121/4719

WAR DIARY

Lucknow Cavalry Brigade.

From 1st February 1915 to 28th February 1915.

Army Form C. 2118.

WAR DIARY
or
INTELLIGENCE SUMMARY.

(Erase heading not required.)

Lucknow Cavalry Brigade

Instructions regarding War Diaries and Intelligence Summaries are contained in F. S. Regs., Part II. and the Staff Manual respectively. Title pages will be prepared in manuscript.

Hour, Date, Place.	Summary of Events and Information.	Remarks and references to Appendices.
1st Feb 1915 HEUCHIN	2.30pm 29-2mm guns from FIEFS to HEUCHIN into billets vacated by U Battery R.H.A.	
13th Feb. HEUCHIN	H.R.H. the PRINCE of WALES into the 1st Brigade as part of the 1st Indian Cav. Div.	
13th – 28th Feb. HEUCHIN	No change. Regimental, Brigade and Divisional Training being carried out.	

121/5114

WAR DIARY

with Appendices.

Lucknow Cavalry Brigade.

From 1st March 1915 to 31st March 1915

Army Form C. 2118.

Lucknow Cavalry Brigade

WAR DIARY
or
INTELLIGENCE SUMMARY.

(Erase heading not required.)

Instructions regarding War Diaries and Intelligence Summaries are contained in F. S. Regs., Part II, and the Staff Manual respectively. Title pages will be prepared in manuscript.

Hour, Date, Place.	Summary of Events and Information.	Remarks and references to Appendices.
1st March 1915 HEUCHIN	No change	
2nd March 3rd " 4th " }	Brigade sends 600 men daily to construct main trenches to rightabout ST VENANT — ROBECQ	
7th March FEBVIN	Bde. moves at 6.45 p.m. to clear billets. H.Q. and K.D.G.: FEBVIN; 29th Lancers FONTAINE LEZ HERMANS; 36th J. Horse PALFART and LIVOSSART.	
8th, 9th March FEBVIN 10th March " 11th March Bois des Dames	No change. Bde. orders 5th inst. to move at an hour's notice. Bde. marched at 4.30 a.m. via PERNES to MARLES to BOIS DES DAMES (nr LAPUGNOY) where, with the remainder of the 1st Indian Cavalry, it bivouacks in a concealed position in the woods. Patrols were sent to reconnoitre the exits of the woods to the S.E. and the route to ANNE QUIN. Transport meanwhile is MARLES until the evening when it rejoins at BDR. No guards along horse lines and front of resting MARJLES — LA BEUVRIERE	App. 1 & 2

Army Form C. 2118.

WAR DIARY
or
INTELLIGENCE SUMMARY.   LUCKNOW Cavalry Brigade

(Erase heading not required.)

Instructions regarding War Diaries and Intelligence Summaries are contained in F. S. Regs., Part II, and the Staff Manual respectively. Title pages will be prepared in manuscript.

Hour, Date, Place.	Summary of Events and Information.	Remarks and references to Appendices.
11th March Cont?	The Bde. remained at 1 hour notice to move transport to day. Bde. bivouacked for the night in the woods. Weather mild and fine.	
12th March AUCHEL	Bde. remained in BOIS DES DAMES until 12.30 p.m. and then marched to AUCHEL and went into billets there. Stew at 1 hour notice to move. Weather mild and fine.	App. 3 + 4
13th March AUCHEL 14th March AUCHEL	Bde. ordered to march back and billet in area FLECHIN – FEBVIN. Transport moves at 9.30 p.m.	App. 5 + 6
15th March FEBVIN	Bde. marched at 12.30 am. & reached its billets at 5 am. Distribution as follows Bde H.Q. & 36th Jacobs Horse FEBVIN; K Dys BONCOURT – CUHEM – part of FLECHIN; 29th Lancers PIPPEMONT and part of FLECHIN.	App. 7 + 8
16th March LIGNY-LEZ-AIRE	Bde. H.Q. moves to LIGNY LEZ AIRE billets at FEBVIN being insanitary.	
17th March LIGNY	Bde. now extend the ready & move at 4 hrs notice. H.Q. & 2 Squadrons 29th Lancers move to LA TIRNAND evacuating PIPPEMONT as insanitary.	

J. Vaughan

Army Form C. 2118.

WAR DIARY or INTELLIGENCE SUMMARY.

Lucknow Cavalry Brigade

(Erase heading not required.)

Instructions regarding War Diaries and Intelligence Summaries are contained in F. S. Regs., Part II, and the Staff Manual respectively. Title pages will be prepared in manuscript.

Hour, Date, Place.	Summary of Events and Information.	Remarks and references to Appendices.
18th March LIETTRES	Bde with remainder of 1st Ind. Cav. Div. inspected by G.O.C. Ind. Cav. Corps. Bde moved to new Billets on afternoon - Bde H.Q. LIETTRES, 36th Horse LINGHEM and LIETTRES, 29th Lancers ESTREE BLANCHE and FLECHINELLE, K.D.G. stood fast at CUHEM, FLECHIN and BONCOURT	
19th March – 31st March LIETTRES	No change	

J. Anson Bingham
Brigade Major
Lucknow

SECRET   Lucknow Bde   Copy No 7
                                                     app 1.

OPERATION ORDER No 1

By MAJOR GENERAL H.D. FANSHAWE, C.B.,

Commanding 1st Indian Cavalry Division.

Headquarters, 1st Ind: Cav: Division.
10th March 1915.

Reference Map $\frac{1}{80,000}$

1.   The Division will march to BOIS-DES-DAMES as follows :-

Sialkot Brigade Starting point BELLERY at 4.30 a.m., Route FERFAY - CAUCHY - A la TOUR - CAMBLAIN - CHATELAIN - MARLES — LA BEUVRIERE.

Lucknow Brigade. Starting point NEDONCHELLE Church at 4.30 a.m., Route AUMERVAL - PERNES - CAMBLAIN - CHATELAIN - MARLES.-

Ambala Brigade Starting point FEBVIN at 4.30 a.m., Route FEBVIN - FONTAINE - LEZ - HERMANS - NEDON-CHELLE and thereafter as for Lucknow Brigade.

Troops will be in BOIS DES DAMES by 8.0 AM

2.   Transport. (a) Transport of Sialkot Brigade will follow its brigade along the main AUCHY - AU - BOIS, FERFAY, CAUCHY CAMBLAIN - CHATELAIN road to MARLES and LABEUVRIERE and will park in the BOIS DES DAMES with its Brigade.

(b) Transport of Lucknow and Ambala Brigades will follow in the order mentioned in rear of the Ambala Brigade and will park at MARLES, the Lucknow Brigade transport will turn to the left in MARLES up the LOZINGHEM road and park North of the railway crossing - The Ambala Brigade transport will turn to the right in MARLES and park on the LABUISSIERE road South of the railway.

(c) The Divisional Troops transport will march to MARLES at the same hour and at the head of the Divisional Ammunition Column (See para 3) - Route AMES, BELLERY, AUMERVAL, PERNES, CAMBLAIN - CHATELAIN, MARLES.

3. Divisional Ammunition Column, S.A.A., Section. The Divisional Ammunition Column will march to AUCHEL al 7.30 a.m., Starting point Bridge under LIERES - LILLERS railway on ST HILAIRE - LIERES road. Route AMES, BELLERY, AUMERVAL, PERNES, FLORINGHEM, CAUCHY, AUCHEL.

4. Medical. Lucknow Field Ambulance (Less motor ambulance) only will accompany the Division and will follow the Divisional Ammunition Column to AUCHEL Motor ambulances of the Lucknow Field Ambulance will proceed to AUCHEL at 9.0 a.m.,

Sialkot and Ambala Field Ambulances will remain in billets.

5. Field Squadron. The Field Squadron will remain in its present billets.

6. Reports. Report centre will be opened at MARLES at 7.0 a.m.,

R.o'B.Taylor
Lieut: Colonel,
General Staff,
1st Indian Cavalry Division.

Issued at 7.35 p.m.,

Operation order 1 Copy No. 8
by
Br. Genl. W. H. Fasken   app. 2.
Comdg Lucknow Cavy Bde
10.3.1915

1. The Brigade will march tomorrow morning to vicinity of MARLES via FONTAINE-LEZ-HERMANS — AUMERVAL — PERNES — CAMBLAIN CHATELAIN.
Starting Point NEDONCHELLE CHURCH at 4.30 AM.

2. (a) Order of march as under
   A.G (name of Comdr to be   1 Sqdn 29th Lancers.
       submitted at S.P)

   Main Body   29th L. (less 1 Sqdn)
                K D Gs.
                36th J.H. (less 2 troops)
                2nd & 3rd chargers of whole Bde.
                Regimental Reserve Ammunition.

   Rear Guard.   1 Troop 36th J.H.

   (b) O.C. 36th J.H. will detail 1 Troop to report to Bde Major at Starting Point. These men will be dropped en route for closing roads and will rejoin Rearguard when Bde has passed.

3. 'A' Echelon Transport less Regimental Reserve Amtn. under an officer to be detailed by O.C. K D Gs and 'B' Echelon Transport under 1 officer or Interpreter per unit will each march in order of units the whole under the Bde Transport Officer. Both echelons will be in rear of the AMBALA Bde and in front of the AMBALA Bde Transport. Head of 'A' Echelon to be at Bde Starting Point at 6.15 am.

"A" Form. Army Form C. 2121.

MESSAGES AND SIGNALS.

No. of Message _____

Prefix	Code	m.	Words	Charge		Recd. at	m.
Office of Origin and Service Instructions.					*This message is on a/c of:	Date	
			Sent				
At _____ m.					Service.	From	
To							
By					(Signature of "Franking Officer.")	By	

TO —

Sender's Number	Day of Month	In reply to Number	AAA

From _____
Place _____
Time _____

*The above may be forwarded as now corrected. (Z)

Censor. Signature of Addressor or person authorised to telegraph in his name

*This line should be erased if not required.

II

KDG Transport will ensure that the FLÉCHIN — FEBVIN, LIGNY — FEBVIN and FEBVIN — FONTAINE LEZHERMANS roads are kept clear for the fighting portion of AMBALA BDE to pass.

29th Lancers will similarly keep the FONTAINE LEZ HERMANS — AUMERVAL road clear.

4. Reports to Head of main Body.

10.20 p.m. J. Mumford Capt
                    Bde Major.

Copy No 1   to KDG   by Orderly   at 10.30 pm
  "   " 2   " 29 L   " Motor Cycle   "
  "   " 3   " 36 H   "   "   "
  "   " 4   " Bde Tpt Offr personally   "
  "   " 5   " Sig. Troop   "   "
  "   " 6   " Mob: Vety Sec   "   "
  "   " 7, 8   Bde Staff.

"A" Form.
Army Form C. 2121

MESSAGES AND SIGNALS.

No. of Message _____

Prefix	Code	m.	Words	Charge		This message is on a/c of:	Recd. at	m.
Office of Origin and Service Instructions.			Sent At ___ m. To By			Service. (Signature of "Franking Officer.")	Date From By	

TO

Sender's Number	Day of Month	In reply to Number	AAA

From
Place
Time

The above may be forwarded as now corrected. (Z)

Censor. Signature of Addressor or person authorised to telegraph in his name

This line should be erased if not required.

MESSAGES AND SIGNALS.

Army Form C. 2121.

app 3

TO: SIALKOT, AMBALA, LUCKNOW — Cav Bde

Sender's Number: G.A. 162 Day of Month: 12th AAA

Division will move into billets as follows: AMBALA Bde will march to CAUCHY A LA TOUR and FLORINGHEM via CALONNE-RICOUART at 11 A.M and with its transport will be clear off of turning to AUCHEL ½ Mile North West of 1st C of CALONNE-RICOUART by 1 p.m AAA LUCKNOW Bde will march at 12.30 p.m to AUCHEL via the turning abovementioned and with its transport will be clear of MARLES village by 2 p.m AAA SIALKOT Bde will not pass the L of LAPUGNOY till 1.45 P.M and will billet in MARLES. AAA Final rendezvous for Supply Column is the north end of RAIMBERT at 3.0 P.M

From: 1st Ind Cav Div
Time: 9.50 P.M

"A" Form.   Army Form C. 2121.
MESSAGES AND SIGNALS.   No. of Message

Prefix ___ Code ___ m | Words | Charge | | Recd. at ___ m
Office of Origin and Service Instructions. | | This message is on a/c of: | Date
                      | Sent | | | From
                      | At ___ m: | | Service.|
                      | To | | |
                      | By | (Signature of "Franking Officer.") | By

TO { K.D.Yo Sig Y
     2 D. G.   G Y
     3 D. G. III M.G.

| Sender's Number | Day of Month | In reply to Number | AAA |
| P.M.13 | 12 | | |

1. The Bde is to go into billets at AUCHEL
2. The Bde will march to AUCHEL via HAILLICOURT –
   CAUCHY – RICOUART, starting Point 1/9 RUITZ
   Station (½ mile W of present Bde H.Q.) — 12.30 p.m
3. Order of march
   A.C. 10, w 36 H.H
   M.G. 3rd J.H. 4th & 5th
   K.D.Yo
   2 G. Lancers
   2nd & 3rd chargers of whole Bde
   Regtal Reserve Ammunition
   B Echelon
   B Echelon

4. O.C. K.D.Yo will detail an officer to be i/charge
   of R.E. station & 3rd Horses, an officer i/charge of
   2nd & 3rd chargers
5. Rear of transport to be clear of MAISNIL by 2 p.m

From   Reports to Head of M.B.
Place
Time   10.30 a.m

"A" Form.　　　　　　　　　　　　　　　Army Form C. 2121.
MESSAGES AND SIGNALS.　　No. of Message _____

Prefix ___ Code ___ m.	Words.	Charge.	This message is on a/c of:	Recd. at 5 ___ m.
Office of Origin and Service Instructions.		Sent		Date ___
Priority	At ___ m.		___ Service.	From ___
	To ___			By ___
	By ___		(Signature of "Franking Officer.")	

TO { Sialkot)   ADMS   OC Ammn Park
     Ambala } Brigades   CRE   OC Signal Sqdn
     Lucknow)   OC ASC

Sender's Number: Q1421　Day of Month: 14　In reply to Number:　　AAA

Brigades will move into new billets as follows: Billeting parties should be despatched at once.
Sialkot Brigade   ST HILARE - COTTES - LIERES
Ambala Brigade   FONTAINE - LES - HERMANS - NEDONCHELLE - NEDON - AMETTES.
Lucknow Brigade   CUHEM - FLECHIN - BONCOURT - PIPPEMONT - FEBVIN.
Divisional H.Q.   BOURECQ.
Field Ambulances   DITTO
Signal Squadron   DITTO.
Field Sqd & Troop   LESPESSES
Ammunition Col.   WESTREHEM

From: 1st Ind Cavalry Division
Place:
Time: 4.0 p

The above may be forwarded as now corrected. (Z)   McBorron   Major
　　　　　　　　　　　　Censor. Signature of Addressee or person authorised to telegraph in his name
* This line should be erased if not required.

COPY NO. 7 *Lucknow Bde app 6*

OPERATION ORDER No. 2

BY MAJOR GENERAL H.D. FANSHAWE, C.B.,

COMMANDING 1st INDIAN CAVALRY DIVISION.

Headquarters, 14th March 1915.

1. The Division will return to its billeting area tonight as follows :-

Lucknow Brigade will march to its billeting area CUHEM - FLECHIN - BONCOURT - PIPPEMONT - FEBVIN via CAUCHY, FLORINGHEM, PERNES, AUMERVAL, NEDONCHELLE and will be clear of FLORINGHEM by 2.0 a.m., its transport will be clear of CAUCHY - FERFAY and CAUCHY - FLORINGHEM cross roads by 11.0 p.m., and NEDONCHELLE by 2.30 a.m.,

Ambala Brigade will march to its billeting area FONTAINE-LEZ-HERMANS, NEDONCHELLE, NEDON- AMETTES. Starting point FLORINGHEM Church at 3.0 a.m., and will proceed via AUMERVAL followed by its transport.

Sialkot Brigade will march to its billeting area ST HILAIRE, COTTES, LIERES via CAUCHY, FERFAY, AMES. The Brigade transport will not be at CAUCHY - FERFAY and CAUCHY - FLORINGHEM cross roads before 11.0 p.m., and will be clear by midnight. The Brigade will be in its billeting area by 6.0 a.m., but will not pass the CAUCHY cross roads before 3.0 a.m.,

Divisional Troops.
(Commander, Major Bremner, R.E.,)
Field Ambulances --- RELY.

Divisional Ammunition Column
(S. A. A., Section) --- WESTREHEM.

Field Squadron --- LESPESSES.

{ In the order mentioned will march to the places named passing the CAUCHY-FERFAY & CAUCHY-FLORINGHEM cross roads at 10.0 p.m.; }

2. REPORTS. Brigades will report by 9.0 a.m., the time of arrival and their headquarters.

Divisional Headquarters will open at BOURECQ at 8.30 a.m., and close here at the same hour.

Conway-Endon Major
for Lieut: Colonel,
General Staff,
1st Indian Cavalry Division.

Issued at 5.15 p.m.,

"A" Form. Army Form C. 2121.

MESSAGES AND SIGNALS.   No. of Message _____

Prefix _____ Code _____ m. | Words | Charge | This message is on a/c of: | Recd. at _____ m.
Office of Origin and Service Instructions. | Sent | | | Date _____
 | At _____ m. | | Service. | From _____
 | To | | |
 | By | | (Signature of "Franking Officer.") | By _____

TO | K.D.G. | 29 L. | 36 J.H.

Sender's Number | Day of Month | In reply to Number | AAA
Bm 25 | 14 | |

Billets are allotted as follows :—

Bde HQ. & 36th H. FEBVIN
K.D.G. BOWCOURT, CUHEM and
FLECHIN west, i.e. both sides
of BOWCOURT–FLECHIN and
FLECHIN–CUHEM roads

29 L. PIPPEMONT and FLECHIN
East, i.e. both sides of roads running
north of from FLECHIN & in "E"
of FLECHIN & of FLECHIN–
FEBVIN road

Billeting parties will leave at once.
A Staff Officer will be at FLECHIN
to divide up the village to parties
detailed

From | B.M.
Place |
Time | 4.45 p.m.

The above may be forwarded as now corrected. (Z)

Censor. Signature of Addressor or person authorised to telegraph in his name
* This line should be erased if not required.

Operation Order No 2
by
B. Genl. [Roth Faskin]
Comdg Lucknow Cav. Bde.

Copy No 7

4.3.15

1. The Bde will march during the night to its billets as allotted in BM 25 of date. Route to be followed: CAUCHY - FLORINGHEM - BLARINGHEM - AUMERVAL - NEDONCHELLE

2. The Transport of the Brigade will march tonight at 9.30pm. Starting point AUCHEL Church. Order of march as under:
   K D Gs
   29th Lancers
   36th J. H.
   Bde H. Q.

Both echelons including Regimental Reserve ammunition & third chargers of each unit will march together under a British Officer of the unit.

3. The Brigade will march at 12.30am 15th instant. Starting point AUCHEL church. Order of march as under:
   A.G.   1 Squadron K D. Gs
   M.B.   KDGs less 1 Squadron
           29th Lancers
           36th J. H. (less 2 troops)
           2nd chargers of Bde under a B.O
           to be detailed by 36th J H
   R.G.   1 Troop 36th J. H.

4. O.C 36th J H will detail 1 troop under a B.O. start at 11.30pm & drop men to block roads, to rejoin rearguard.

5. Report to Head of M.B. after 12.15 am
   6.45 p.m.

121/5504

Copy No. 777

WAR DIARY
OF
Lucknow Cavalry Brigade.

From 1st April 1915 to 30th April 1915

April 1915

WAR DIARY
INTELLIGENCE SUMMARY

LUCKNOW Cavalry Brigade

Army Form C. 2118.

(Erase heading not required.)

Instructions regarding War Diaries and Intelligence Summaries are contained in F.S. Regs., Part II. and the Staff Manual respectively. Title pages will be prepared in manuscript.

Hour, Date, Place.	Summary of Events and Information.	Remarks and references to Appendices.
1st April LIETTRES	No change	
23rd April		
24th April LIETTRES	Bde. ordered SD at 2 hours notice to move. 5:30 p.m. Bde. concentrates at ESTREE BLANCHE and marched at 7 p.m. towards CASSEL.	App 1 & 2
25th April ½ mile East of ST MARIE CAPPEL	Bde. reached its billets in area S.E. of CASSEL in company with remainder of 1st Indian Cavalry Division. Remained in billets. Provisions & men at 1 hours notice	
25th – 27th April ½ mile East of ST MARIE CAPPEL	No change	
28th April ST JANS TER BIEZEN	Bde. marches at 12:50 p.m. to ST JANS TER BIEZEN, BELGIUM and went into billets there and in immediate vicinity. On 1 hour notice to move continued.	App 3
29th, 30th April ST JANS TER BIEZEN	No change	

[signature]
Br. Major
Lucknow Ca. Bde.

Copy No. 6 app 1.

LUCKNOW

1st Indian Cavalry Division Order No. 3.

Reference $\frac{1}{80,000}$

1. The Division will move on the area South East of the ST OMER – CASSEL road and billet within the limits MAISON BLANCHE, STAPLE, inclusive ST MARIE CAPPEL inclusive – OXELAERE exclusive BAVINCHOVE Station exclusive.

2. Division will march as follows :-

Lucknow Brigade. Railway arch ESTREE BLANCHE at 5.30 p.m., Route BASSEE BOULOGNE, MARTHES, MAMETZ, ROQUETOIRE, forked road ¼ mile North of D in QUISTEDE, BELLECROIX, WARDRECQUES, ERB-LINGHEM, STAPLES, cross roads just west of L in LONGUECROIX where the Staff Captain will meet it.

Sialkot Brigade. Starting point – THEROUANNE 6.20 p.m., Route THEROUANNE, CLARQUES, QUIESTEDE, BELLE CROIX, WARDRECQUES, EBBLINGHEM, LE NIEPPE to MAISON BLANCHE where the Staff Captain will meet it.

Ambala Brigade. Starting point – Church at LIERES at 5.30 p.m. Route ST HILAIRE, Cross roads East of ESTRACELLE, thence via MISSISSIPI, NEUFPRE, PECQUER, M of BOESEGHEM, WALLON CAPPEL to STAPLES.

3. Transport of Lucknow and Sialkot Brigades will follow their Brigades – Starting point as for Brigades at the following times.

LUCKNOW Bde Transport........6.0 p.m.,

SIALKOT Brigade Transport,...7.0 p.m.,

Divisional Headquarters Transport will march at head of Lucknow Brigade Transport.

Transport of AMBALA Brigade will follow Brigade.

4. Divisional Ammunition Column will follow the Ambala Brigade and proceed via LONGUECROIX to ST MARIE CAPELLE.

5. Medical Sialkot Field Ambulance will follow the Divisional Ammunition Column to ST MARIE CAPELLE.
The remainder of F.A. Ambulance will remain in billets
6. Report Centre will close at ENQUIN at 6.0 p.m., and open at ST MARIE CAPELLE at same time.

Norway Inden Major,
General Staff,
1st Indian Cavalry Division.

Operation order No 1. Copy No 6. App. 2

Brigade Machine Gun Coy LCH

Rcf St Omer map   24.4.16

1. Bde marches at once towards
CASSEL, starting point railway
arch ESTRÉE BLANCHE.

2. Order of march
   2 Sqn Lancers
   36 J. Horse
   K } H.Q. Transport
   A Echelon } in order of
   B Echelon } units.

3. Route for Bde BASSE BOULOGNE
— MARTHES — MAMETZ —
ROQUETOIRE — forked road ½
mile north of D in OUESTREDE
— BELLE CROIX — WARDRECQUES
— EBBLINGHEM — STAPLES
— X rds just west of L in
LONGUECROIX.

5.35 p.m.   [signature]
                                Bd...

"A" Form. Army Form C. 2121.
MESSAGES AND SIGNALS. No. of Message _____

Prefix____ Code____ m.	Words.	Charge.	This message is on a/c of:	Recd. at____ m.
Office of Origin and Service Instructions.	Sent At____ m. To____ By____		____Service, (Signature of "Franking Officer.")	Date____ From____ By____

TO {

*	Sender's Number	Day of Month	In reply to Number	AAA

From
Place
Time

The above may be forwarded as now corrected. (**Z**)

Censor. Signature of Addressor or person authorised to telegraph in his name

* This line should be erased if not required.
(24473). M.R.Co.,Ltd. Wt.W4843/541. 50,000. 9/14. Forms C2121/10.

MESSAGES AND SIGNALS.

TO	K.S. 21 L 36 J.H.	B.S.O. B.T.O. M.V.S.

Sender's Number	Day of Month	In reply to Number	AAA
BM 294	25		

1. Sialkot Bde, First Sqn. of R.H.A. are moving to WATOU via RYVELD

2. Lucknow Bde follows R.H.A. to point where RYVELD road branches off main CASSEL-POPERINGHE and then marches independently to ST JANS TER BIEZEN via STEENVOORDE – BEAUVOORDE.

3. Ambala Bde follows Lucknow Bde to RYVELD road junction and then follows route of Sialkot Bde.

4. Starting point LUCKNOW Bde cross at Bde H.Q. Order of march as under

   A.G. one troop 29ᵗʰ Lancers
   M.B. 29ᵗʰ Lancers less 1 troop
        36 J.H.
        K.S.

From A [illegible] in order of march.
Place 5. Repairs ahead of M.B.
Time 12.15 p—

Serial No. 111.

121/5799

WAR DIARY
with appendices.

Lucknow Cavalry Brigade. Hd. Qrs.

From 1st May 1915 to 31st May 1915

May 1915

Army Form C. 2118.

LUCKNOW Cavalry Brigade

WAR DIARY
or
INTELLIGENCE SUMMARY.
(Erase heading not required.)

Instructions regarding War Diaries and Intelligence Summaries are contained in F. S. Regs., Part II, and the Staff Manual respectively. Title pages will be prepared in manuscript.

Hour, Date, Place.	Summary of Events and Information.	Remarks and references to Appendices.
1st May ST JAN TER BIEZEN	Bde remain at own horse's retire to move. Mobile Veterinary Section removed from Brigade and attached to Indian Cavalry Corps Head Quarters	
2nd May ½ mile West of STE MARIE CAPPEL	Bde, with rest of 1st Indian Cavalry Division marches back to previous billeting area south of CASSEL. Bde at 4 hours notice to move	Apps: 1 & 2
3rd May ½ mile West of STE MARIE CAPPEL	No change	
4th May ditto	Bde under orders to move early 5th inst.	
5th May MAMETZ	Bde marched at 2 am and reached billets 5.30 am. Bde billets as follows Bde HQ MAMETZ; K.D.G., RINCQ, WARNE & LA JUMELLE; 29th Lancers MAMETZ & CRECQUES; 36th J. ttwo MARTHES, HAM & BLESSY.	App 3 & 4
6.7.8th May MAMETZ	No change except 1 Squadron K.D.G. sent to Indian Corps front and Bde ordered Bde at 2 hours notice from 5th April. 9th May +	
9 – 12th May MAMETZ	Remained in area upto 5 p.m 12th May when it was put at 4 hours' notice.	
13 – 15th May MAMETZ	No change	

WAR DIARY LUCKNOW Cav Bde.

or

INTELLIGENCE SUMMARY.

(Erase heading not required.)

Army Form C. 2118.

May 1915

Hour, Date, Place.	Summary of Events and Information.	Remarks and references to Appendices.
16th May MAMETZ	Bde at 2 hours notice from 10 am	
17th May LE REVEILLON	Bde marched at 4 p.m. to LE REVEILLON (near ALLOUAGNE) via AIRE & LILLERS. Troops got bivouac & own billets there. A Echelon A.T. Carts returned & bivouacked 6-8 kms in rear.	App 5 & 6
18th May BURBURE	Owing to lack of accommodation at LE REVEILLON Bde moved into clean billets at BURBURE 2.30 p.m.	
19th May MAMETZ	Bde returns to previous billets in MAMETZ area and remains at 4 hours notice. Drawn	App. 7 & 8
20th – 26th May MAMETZ	No change. HQ Km 1.5 WDS brig started to 2nd army 26/5/15	
27th May QUEUE D'OXELAERE	Bde marched to area about QUEUE D'OXELAERE, south of CASSEL.	App 9 & 10
28th May VLAMERTINGHE	Bde marched at 6.30 am to L'ERKELSBRUGGE. Horses and B Echelon were left there and Bde proceeded on to VLAMERTINGHE when Artillery harnessed direct. Troops go into huts & bivouacs S.W. of VLAMERTINGHE.	App 11, 12 & 13

"A" Form.
Army Form C. 2121.
MESSAGES AND SIGNALS. No. of Message

Prefix	Code	m.	Words	Charge	This message is on a/c of:	Recd. at	m.
Office of Origin and Service Instructions.			Sent			Date	
			At	m.		From	
priority			To		Service.		
			By		(Signature of "Franking Officer.")	By	

TO	SIALKOT	I.C.C	C.R.H.A.	A.D.V.S
	AMBALA } Cav Bde		S.R.EO	Camp Comdt
	LUCKNOW		A.D.M.S.	Signal

| Sender's Number. | Day of Month | In reply to Number | |
| G.A.1265 | 1st | | AAA |

The 1st Division will return tomorrow to its previous billeting area round ST MARIE CAPPEL AAA Divisional Starting point the corner of the DROGLANDT - WINNEZEELE - RYVELD road in WATOU main street at 6.0 A.M. AAA order of march AMBALA Bde - LUCKNOW Bde - R.H.A - Field Squadron - SIALKOT Bde - Div Amm Coln - Field Ambulances - AAA on arrival at the junction of POPERINGHE - CASSEL and BAILLEUL - CASSEL main roads units will break off into their old billeting areas AAA B. Echelon transport in order of units will pass the Divisional starting point as above at 8.30 A.M. with Div HQ Transport at the head of column AAA Report Centre will close at WATOU at 6.0 AM and open at ST MARIE CAPPEL at same hour.

From	1st Ind Cav Div			
Place				
Time	9.30 P.M	Conway Indian Major		
	The above may be forwarded as now corrected.	(Z)		
	Censor.	Signature of Addressor or person authorised to telegraph in his name.		

"A" Form.
Army Form C.2121

MESSAGES AND SIGNALS.

This message is on a/c of: App 2 Service.

TO: K.D.G. / 29 L. / 36 J.H. / B.S.O. / B.T.O.

Sender's Number: B.M.311
Day of Month: 1st
AAA

1. The Bde will return to its previous billets South of CASSEL tomorrow.

2. Starting point cross roads at K.D.G. H.Q. (N of "R" of WASANDEBECK) at 6 am. Route WATOU – WINNEZEELE – RYVELD.

3. LUCKNOW Bde follows the AMBALA Bde and is followed by R.H.A. SIALKOT Bde follows R.H.A.

4. Order of march
   K.D.G.
   36 J.H.
   29 Lancers
   A Echelon in order of units.

5. B Echelon will march by same route from same starting at 8 am. order of

"A" Form.
MESSAGES AND SIGNALS.
Army Form C. 2121
No. of Message _____

Prefix ___ Code ___ m.	Words.	Charge.	This message is on a/c of:	Recd. at ___ m.
Office of Origin and Service Instructions.	Sent			Date ___
	At ___ m.		___ Service.	From ___
	To ___			
	By ___		(Signature of "Franking Officer.")	By ___

TO {				

Sender's Number	Day of Month	In reply to Number	**A A A**
		March on for Bde.	
6.	As M.O. vet. Lieut. has left Bde sick horses will march under Farrier Q.M.S. of R.A.S.		
7.	Reports after 5.45 am Head of B.d.		
10.5 p.m.		[signature]	

From _____
Place _____
Time _____

The above may be forwarded as now corrected. **(Z)**

Censor. | Signature of Addressor or person authorised to telegraph in his name

*This line should be erased if not required.

Copy No. 7 opp 3

LUCKNOW

1st Indian Cavalry Division Order No. 4.

Reference 1/80,000

4th May 1915

1. The Division will march to-night to the billeting area North West of AIRE as follows :-

Sialkot Brigade.	Starting point MAISON BLANCHE, 12 midnight. Route - Main road to ARQUES, thence via BLENDECQUES and HEURINGHEM.
	Sialkot Brigade transport will follow the Brigade.
Ambala Brigade.	Will march 12 midnight via EBBLINGHEM and RENESCURE.
	Ambala Brigade transport will follow the Brigade and will be clear of the road south of NG in EBBLENGHEM at 2/30 a.m.,
Lucknow Brigade	Starting point LONGUE CROIX at 2/0 a.m., Route STAPLE, EBBLINGHEM, WARDRECQUES Ston
Field Squadron	will march via HONDEGHEM, to LONGUE CROIX and follow the Lucknow Brigade,
Divl Ammn Column. (S.A.A.Sec:)	Will follow the Field Squadron.
Field Ambulances	(Less motors) will march from STAPLE at 3.30 a.m., and proceed via EBBLINGHEM, WARDRECQUES Ston in rear of Divisional Ammunition Column.
Divl Hq: Transport	will march via HONDEGHEM, LONGUE CROIX, reaching LONGUE CROIX at 3.30 a.m., and will follow the Field Ambulances.

"B" Echelon, Lucknow Brigade will follow the Divisional Headquarters transport.

2. Water carts may accompany "A" echelon.

3. Report centre will close ST MARIE CAPPEL at 7.0 a.m. tomorrow and open at ROQUETOIRE Chau the same hour. Reports of arrival to be sent to ROQUETOIRE Chau.

R.o'B. Taylor Lieut: Colonel,
General Staff.
1st Indian Cavalry Division.

Issued at 6.0 p.m.,

Operation Order No. 2 Copy No. 6
by
Br. Genl. W. H. Larken
Comdg. Lahore Cavy Bde
4-5-15.

1. Bde. will march to billets in the MAMETZ area tonight. The Field Squadron marches in rear of Bde. 'A' Echelon.

2. Starting Point Cross Roads W. of L. of GENEVECHEN at 2 a.m. 5th inst. Route STAPLE – EBBLINGHEM – WARDRECQUES STN – BELLE CROIX. Beyond latter point route of units to their billets will be intimated later.

3. Order of march.
   A.G.   1 Troop KDGs
          1 Troop 29th L.
   M.B.   KDGs less 1 troop
          36th J.H.
          29th L. less 1 troop
          'A' Echelon in order of units
   The troop 29th L. attached to AG is for blocking roads until 'A' Echelon has passed.

4. 'B' Echelon in order of units will march from same S.P. at 3.30 a.m. and will follow Divl. HQ Transport — Water carts will march in 'A' Echelon.

5. Reports to be sent after 1 a.m. to S.P. and on march to Head of Bde.

Issued at 7.35 p.m.

                                    Capt.
                        Bde Major Lahore Cavy Bde

"A" Form. Army Form C. 2121.

MESSAGES AND SIGNALS.   No. of Message _____

Prefix_____ Code_____ m.	Words.	Charge.	This message is on a/c of:	Recd. at_____ m.
Office of Origin and Service Instructions.	Sent			Date_____
_____	At_____ m.		_____ Service.	From_____
_____	To_____			
_____	By_____		(Signature of "Franking Officer.")	By_____

TO { _____

*	Sender's Number	Day of Month	In reply to Number	A A A

From			
Place			
Time			

The above may be forwarded as now corrected.   (Z)

Censor. Signature of Addressor or person authorised to telegraph in his name

* This line should be erased if not required.

(24473). M.R.Co.,Ltd. Wt.W4843/541. 50,000. 9/14. Forms C2121/10.

1st Indian Cavalry Division Order No. 7.

Reference map 1/80,000

17th May 1915.

1. The 1st Army broke the enemy's lines yesterday on the front LA QUINQUE - RUE - RICHEBOURG L'AVOUE.

2. The Indian Cavalry Corps (less "B" Echelon) will move to a position of readiness about LE MARQUET.

3. The Division will march to the area ALLOUAGNE - LE REVEILLON and the Western sides of the BOIS DU REVEILLON and the MARQUET woods via LAMBRES, ST HILAIRE, LILLERS, HAUT RIEUX, as follows :-

Signal Squadron	Starting point the bend in the road just East of the last E of MOULIN LE COMTE at 4.0 p.m.,
LUCKNOW BRIGADE	Starting point as for Signal Squadron at 4.0 p.m.,
Field Squadron.	Marching by the main ST OMER - AIRE Road will join the Column at the road junction ¼ mile East of the last E in ESTRACELLE (500 yards S.W. of AIRE), at 4.45 p.m.,
SIALKOT Brigade.	Starting point as for Signal Squadron at 5.0 p.m.,
AMBALA Brigade	Starting point Road junction ¼ mile east of ESTRACELLE 500 yards S.W., of AIRE at 6.0 p.m., The regiment at HEURINGHEM may use the road COUBRONNE OUIESTEDE, ROQUETOIRE, LA JUMELLE or roads North but not South of that road.
Divl Ammn Column. (S.A.A. Section)	Starting point as for Signal Squadron at 6.25 p.m.,
Field Ambulances (Less Ambala Field Ambulance)	Starting point as for Signal Squadron at 6.30 p.m., Ambala Cavalry Field Ambu will remain open in its present position
Jodhpur Lancers	Less one troop escort to Corps Headquart Starting point the junction of the ROMBI NORRENT FONTES and main AIRE ST HILAIRE roads at 7.30 p.m., and will billet at BURBURE

4. "B" Echelon transport will be brigaded and remain in present billeting area Regimental guards and loading parties will be left in accordance with Corps No. Q-4967 but wagons will not be unloaded till orders are received.

5. Report Centre will close at ROQUETOIRE and 5.0 p.m and open at ALLOUAGNE at same hour.

R. d B. Taylor Lieutenant Colonel
General Staff.

Issued at 3.15 p.m.,

"A" Form.　　　　　　　　　　　　　　　　　　Army Form C. 2121.
MESSAGES AND SIGNALS.　　No. of Message_____

Prefix___ Code___ m.	Words.	Charge.	This message is on a/c of:	Recd. at_____ m.
Office of Origin and Service Instructions.	Sent		a.p.p.	Date 6
_____	At___ m.		_____Service.	From___
_____	To___			By___
_____	By___		(Signature of "Franking Officer.")	

TO { 1st, Archlen
　　　2e
　　　3e

Sender's Number	Day of Month	In reply to Number	AAA
Bm 393	17.		

1. The Bde will march to a position of readiness about LE MARQUET via LAMBRES – ST HILAIRE – LILLERS – HAUT RIEUX. Starting point N.W. corner CHAMPS DE MANOEUVRES (W of AIRE)

2. Order of march
　A. 1 Sqn　2e L
　M.G.　2e L　in 1 Sqn
　K.E.L.
　　3e J H
　Archlen in rear front.

3. The Bde will send to Div Sig Sqn a.
Hourly Fd Sqn & each Bn.

4. Archlen wagons will be inspected at M.H.F. 2 under BATO.

From　Bm
Place
Time
The above may be forwarded as now corrected. (Z)

Censor.　Signature of Addressee or person authorised to telegraph in his name

Copy No. 7

1st Indian Cavalry Division Order No. 6.

19th May 1915.

Reference map 1/80,000

1. The Division will return to its original billeting area at once, as follows -

Lucknow Brigade   will march at 1.45 p.m., via HURIONVILLE, ECQUEDECQUES, BOURECQ, and thence via the road they came to billets.

Signal Sqdn   will march at 2.15 p.m.

Ambala Brigade   Will march at 2.15 p.m., via HAUTRIEUX and LILLERS AIRE main road to billets.

Sialkot Brigade   will march at 3.15 p.m., by the same road as the Ambala Brigade to their billets.

Field Squadron (Less "A" Echelon) will follow the Sialkot Brigade

Divisional Ammn. Col: (S.A.A., Section) will follow the Field Squadron.

Field Squadron "A" Echelon Transport   (In the order
Field Ambulances (Less motors)   ) mentioned will
                                         follow the Divisional Ammunition Column.

2. Report centre will close at ALLOUAGNE at 3.0 p.m., and open at Chateau ROQUETOIRE at same hour.

R. O'B. Taylor
Lieut: Colonel,
General Staff.

Issued at 1.15 p.m.;

"A" Form.   Army Form C. 2121.
MESSAGES AND SIGNALS.   No. of Message _____

Prefix ___ Code ___ m.	Words.	Charge.	This message is on a/c of:	Recd. at ___ m.
Office of Origin and Service Instructions.				Date ___
	Sent		Service.	From ___
	At ___ m.			
	To ___			By ___
	By ___		(Signature of "Franking Officer.")	

TO { KOL / 2E-J / 3E-JV }   2 - Men

| Sender's Number | Day of Month | In reply to Number | AAA |
| * BM 404 | 19 | | |

1. Bde will return to its former billets in MAMETZ area.
2. Route ECQUEDECQUES — BOURECQ — and main AIRE road. Units & transport will break off independently to billets from N.W. corner AIRE. Starting Point HURIONVILLE railway crossing at 1.50 p.m.
3. Order of march
   Adv 1 troop KOL
   MB KOL less 1 troop
   3E- JV
   2E- J
   A column in order of units
4. Reports to Bde HQ 8.1.30 p.m. after that to head of M.B.
5. Bde will still be at 2 hrs. notice after arrival at billets.

From
Place
Time

Copy No. 7.

1st Indian Cavalry Divisional Order No. 7.

26th May 1915.

Reference map 1/80,000

1. The Division will march tomorrow to the area LONGUE CROIX, QUEUE D'OXELAERE, EYHOUCK, LE NIEPPE, EBBLINGHEM, as follows :-

Ambala Brigade "A" Battery R.H.A.,	Starting point. LE PONT DE CAMPAGNE north east of CAMPAGNE at 9.30 a.m., Route - RENESCURE, LA CROSSE and thence by main road to EYHOUCK.
Sialkot Brigade "Q" Battery R.H.A..	Starting point. CAUCHIE D'ECQUES at 9.0 a.m.. Route WARDRECQUES Ston, EBBLINGHEM.
Lucknow Brigade "U" Battery R.H.A.	Starting point. ROQUETOIRE East at 9.30 a.m., Route LE MONTDUPIL, BLARINGHEM, LYNDE, WALLON CAPPEL to QUEUE D'OXELAERE.
Divl Signal Sqdn Divl Amm: Col: (S.A.A., Section) Field Ambulances (Less Ambala C.F.A)	Starting point Road junction north of the last E in OUISTEDE at 8.0 a.m. Route BELLE CROIX, WARDRECQUES Ston, EBBLINGHEM, to STAPLE.
Hq: 1st Indian R.H.A Brigade Divl Amm: Column. (R.H.A.Section) Field Troop, S.& M.	Will follow the Lucknow Brigade to WALLON CAPPEL and thence to STAPLE.

2. "B" Echelon Transport will follow the routes allotted to Brigades.

Divl Hq: "A" & "B" Echelons. Divl Sig: Sq: "B" Echelon. Field Ambulances. "B" Echelon.	Will march in rear of Sialkot Brigade "A" Echelon as far as EBBLINGHEM and thence to STAPLE. It will be at the road junction North of the last E of OUSESTEDE at 10 a.m.

3. Ambala Cavalry Field Ambulance will remain open here tomorrow and will rejoin under further instructions.

4. Report Centre will open at STAPLE at 10.0 a.m., and close here at same hour.

R.o.B. Taylor Lieut: Colonel,
General Staff.
1st Indian Cavalry Division.

Issued 5.30 p.m.,

App 10

Copy No. 7

Operation Order No. 3
by
Brig-Genl W.H.Fasken, Comdg Lucknow Cav. Bde.

Reference ST OMER Map.   26-5-15.

1.   The Brigade will march tomorrow to QUEUE D'OXELAERE via
ROQUETOIRE East — LE MONTDUPIL — BLARINGHEM — LYNDE — WALLON CAPPEL.

2.   Starting Point for Brigade ROQUETOIRE East at 9-30 a.m.

        Preliminary Starting Point for 29th Lancers and 36th Jacob's
Horse cross roads ½ mile North of MAMETZ at 9 a.m.

        A Echelon of both regiments in rear of 36th J.Horse.

        'U' Battery R.H.A. and K.D.Gds at point where LA JUMELLE road
enters Roquetoire East at 9-25 a.m.

3.   Order of March:-

        A.G.   1 sqdn K.D.Gds

        M.B.   K.D.Gds (less 1 sqdn).
                'U' Battery R.H.A.
                29th Lancers.
                36th Jacob's Horse.
                A. Echelon (in order of units).

4.   B Echelon in order of units will assemble under Bde T.O. at
ROQUETOIRE East at 10 a.m. and will follow the same route as the Brigade.

5.   Reports to Bde H.Qrs MAMETZ, ~~till~~ up to 8-30 a.m., after that
to head of Main Body.

                                            S. Thompson Captain.

By Despatch Rider.

7-50 p.m   Brigade Major, Lucknow Cavalry Brigade.

1st Indian Cavalry Divisional Order No. 8.

27th May 1915.

Reference map 1/80,000

1. The Division will march tomorrow to billeting area West of the line NOORDPEENE - SEINEHOUCK and East of the road L'ERRELSBRUGGE - LEDERZEELE as follows :-

Sialkot Brigade (less "A" Echelon)	Starting point LE NIEPPE at 8.0 a.m., Route Cross roads south of B in HAUT-SCHOUBROUCK, L'HEY and thence via Ste ANNE Fe, OOSTHOUCK, BUYSSHEURE, POINT DU JOUR.
Lucknow Brigade. (Less "A" Echelon)	Will march via LONGUE CROIX, STAPLE, MAISON BLANCHE, road junction north of L'HEY, RUBROUCK, to L'ERKELSBRUGGE. The rear of the brigade (Inclusive of its "B" Echelon) will be clear of LONGUE CROIX by 7.0 a.m., and clear of road junction north of L'HEY at 8.30 a.m.,
Ambala Brigade. (Less "A" Echelon).	Starting point - MAISON BLANCHE at 9.15 a.m., Route via cross roads north of L'HEY to NOORD PEENE.

"A" Echelon of the above three brigades and Lucknow Cavalry Field Ambulance will be east of LONGUE CROIX cross roads by 6.0 a.m., and march via LA BREARDE, St SYLVESTRE, STEENVOORDE, POPERINGHE, to BRANDHOEK, ½ mile west of VLAMERTINGHE.

Divisional Troops. (Commander for march purposes - Major Bremner, R.E.)	Divisional Signal Squadron. "A" Echelon, Divl Headquarters. 1st Indian R.H.A. Brigade. Divisional Ammunition Column. Field Troop (Less "A" Echelon) Field Squadron. Field Ambulances (Less Lucknow Cav: Field Ambulance) "A" Echelon, Field Troop.

Will march in the order mentioned above at 10.0 a.m., Starting point MAISON BLANCHE and proceed via cross roads north of L'HEY to RUBROUCK.

2. "B" Echelon Divisional Troops will follow the "A" Field Troop.

"B" Echelon, Lucknow Brigade	Will follow "B" Echelon, Divisional Troops.
"B" Echelon, Ambala Brigade	Will have its head at MAISON BLANCHE at 10.45 a.m., and follow Lucknow Brigade's "B" Echelon as far as the NOORDPEENE road.
"B" Echelon, Sialkot Brigade.	Will have its head at the cross roads north of L'HEY at 11.45 a.m., and when Ambala Brigade's "B" Echelon has cleared it will proceed to its billeting area via the road followed by its brigade.

3 Report centre will close at STAPLE at 9.0 a.m., and open at ROURBROUCK at the same hour.

Issued at 7.30 p.m.,   Lieutenant Colonel, General Staff, 1st Ind: Cav: D

Operation Order No. 4   Copy No.
by Brig-Genl W.H. PASKEN, Comdg Lucknow Cav. Bde
27-5-15.

Reference ST OMER Map. + Hazebrouck

1. Bde less A Echelon will march tomorrow to billeting area about L'ERKELSBRUGGE where horses will be left prior to a bus movement Eastward.
2. Route for Bde STAPLE, MAISON BLANCHE, road junction north of L'HEY, RUBROUCK, Starting Point LONGUE CROIX Cross roads 6-30 a.m.
3. Order of March:-
    A.G. — 1 sqdn K.D.Gds.
    M.B. — K.D.Gds less 1 sqdn.
          36th J. Horse.
          29th Lancers.
4. A Echelon, less led horses, will march independently to BRANDOEK (½ mile West of VLAMERTINGHE) via LA BREARDE, ST SYLVESTRE, STEENVOORDE, POPERINGHE. Starting Point Cross roads due south of N of HONDEGHEM at 5-50 a.m.
5. B Echelon, order of march as for Bde, will march by same route as Bde, Starting Point LONGUE CROIX Cross roads at 6-15 a.m. It will march off ahead of Bde which will afterwards pass it on the road. Rear of B Echelon is to be clear of road junction north of L'HEY by 8-30 a.m.
6. All officers chargers and led horses which can move at a trot will accompany Bde. Sick horses which cannot trot will accompany B Echelon in charge of S.V.O.
7. The Bde will not see its horses or B Echelon so long as it remains in the YPRES neighbourhood. Men will take one blanket and one waterproof sheet with them in the busses. They will probably have to bivouack.
8. Reports to 6-15 a.m. to Bde H.Q. after that hour to head of Main Body.

                                      Captain.
            Bde Major, Lucknow Cav. Bde.

"A" Form.
MESSAGES AND SIGNALS.

Army Form C. 2121.

No. of Message _____

Prefix _____ Code _____ m.	Words	Charge		
Office of Origin and Service Instructions.			*This message is on a/c of:*	Recd. at _____ m.
_____	Sent		_____ Service.	Date _____
_____	At _____ m.			From _____
_____	To _____			
_____	By _____		(Signature of "Franking Officer.")	By _____

TO {

Sender's Number.	Day of Month	In reply to Number	A A A

From _____
Place _____
Time _____

The above may be forwarded as now corrected. (Z)

....
Censor. Signature of Addressee or person authorised to telegraph in his name.

* This line should be erased if not required.

(632) —McS. & Co. Ltd., London.— W 11400/2045. 100,000. 2/15. Forms C 2121/10.

B.M.452.   28.5.191..

1. The Bde will bus from L'ERKELSBRUGGE starting at 2 p.m.

2. Route ZEGGERS CAPPEL, ESQUELBECQ, WORMHOUDT, HERZEELE, ST JAN TER BIEZEN, POPERINGHE to BRANDHOEK ½ mile West of VLAMERTINGHE.

3. There will be 33 busses for Bde, divided as under:-

    Bde H.Qrs and Sig Troop   1
    K.D.Gds   11
    ..th Lancers   10½
    36th J.Horse   10½

Busses take 25 persons each

4. M.G's and Regtl S.A.A.reserve will be taken in busses.

5. 1 blanket and 1 waterproof sheet per man will be taken.

6. Each officer and man will take a gauze veiling respirator. M.G.Detachments, officers and as many N.C.O's as possible will take masks in addition.

7. Detailed orders re embussing points will be given at L'ERKELSBRUGGE.

                              Captain.
Brigade Major, Lucknow Cavalry Brigade.

"A" Form. Army Form C. 2121.

MESSAGES AND SIGNALS.   No. of Message_____

Prefix____ Code____ m.	Words.	Charge.	This message is on a/c of:	Recd. at____ m.
Office of Origin and Service Instructions.				Date____
	Sent		_____Service.	From____
	At____ m.			
	To____			By____
	By____		(Signature of "Franking Officer.")	

TO {

| Sender's Number | Day of Month | In reply to Number | A A A |

From
Place
Time

The above may be forwarded as now corrected.   (Z).

Censor.   Signature of Addressor or person authorised to telegraph in his name

* This line should be erased if not required.

(24473). M.R.Co.,Ltd. Wt.W4843/541. 50,000. 9/14. Forms C2121/10.

Serial No. 111

121/6125

WAR DIARY
OF
Lucknow Cavalry Brigade.

From 1st June 1915. To 30th June 1915.

Army Form C. 2118.

JUNE 1915. WAR DIARY LUCKNOW Cav Bde
or
INTELLIGENCE SUMMARY.

Instructions regarding War Diaries and Intelligence
Summaries are contained in F. S. Regs., Part II,
and the Staff Manual respectively. Title pages
will be prepared in manuscript.

(Erase heading not required.)

Hour, Date, Place.	Summary of Events and Information.	Remarks and references to Appendices.
1st June VLAMERTINGHE	Major R.S. HUNT, K.D.G., wounded during night 31st May – 1st June, no further casualties reported. 10 men 36th J. Horse employed in evening carrying R.E. stores up to 6th & 8th Cav Bde trenches. British and Indian officers of 29th Lancers & 36th J. Horse sent into trenches of 6th Bde for 24 hours spell.	
2nd June VLAMERTINGHE	K.D.G.s at HOOGE together with the 6th & 8th Car Bde in the YPRES salient heavily shelled with high explosives during afternoon. At 6 p.m. Bde placed at disposal P.P.O.C. 3rd Cav Div. and stands to, ready to march up to YPRES at 9 p.m. Bde then K.D.G. arrives to remain in positions at ½ hour notice to move. K.D.G. relieved by LINCOLNS during night 2nd/3rd and marches back to VLAMERTINGHE at × Officer ranks 16 wounded, 20 below, 49 wounded 12 missing. Casualty officers 1 killed x 6 wounded. 3rd Cav. Div. The Bde placed at disposal of G.O.C. 3rd Cav Div.	× Capt RENTON killed. Maj. HUNT, Capts COOPER, ALEXANDER, Lt CARLETON-SMITH, MURRAY JOHNSON, and Capt DICKSON (R.A.M.C.) wounded.
3rd June East of YPRES	3rd Cav Div's 9889 reinforce and on 1st's Bde, Cav KDGs marches at 9 p.m. via YPRES, SALLY PORT to YEOMANRY POST. Gas from asphyxiating shells encountered in YPRES. Respirators found effective and only a few temporarily incapacitated.	
4th June YEOMANRY POST & G.H.Q. line trenches	Bde reaches YEOMANRY POST, 3/4 mile S.W. of HOOGE at 12.30 am and G.O.C. reports at H.Q. Dugout 12.45 a.m.	

WAR DIARY or INTELLIGENCE SUMMARY

Army Form C. 2118.

N CANSW Cavalry Bde

June 1915

Hour, Date, Place.	Summary of Events and Information.	Remarks and references to Appendices.
4th June continued	On orders from 3rd Cav. Div. 150 rifles & 2 M.G. of 36th J. Horse remained at YEOMANRY Post with instructions to inform Sjenen Narska. Remainder of Bde. marched back to B.Q.H.Q. and occupied trenches on East bank of ZILLEBEKE Lake, Bde H.Q. in dug out to west of E. type line. Situation was completed by 2 a.m. Relieve must have been by S.H.E. & shrapnel also during relief. Casualties 7; 12 men, 2 Officers & ranch Jacobs Horse wounds. Aeroplanes informed after dark.	
5th June dito	Some shrapnel in E.H.Q. line in morning. Rest of day otherwise quiet. 8th Cav Bde 100 yards away RA trench & streets. Men began 10:30 p.m. and was clear of ECOLE DE BIEN FAISANCE by 11:30 p.m.	
6th June VLAMERTINGHE	Bde reached VLAMERTINGHE 1 a.m. No further casualties.	
7th June dito	29th Lancers bivouacs in brick fields ½ mile west of VLAMERTINGHE shelled with H.E. at 8.30 p.m. and 9.30 p.m. Men cleared into ditches + trenches outside bivouacs. No casualties amongst personnel. One draught horse and one mule killed.	

Army Form C. 2118.

WAR DIARY
or
INTELLIGENCE SUMMARY.

June 1915.   LUCKNOW Cavalry Brigade

(Erase heading not required.)

Hour, Date, Place.	Summary of Events and Information.	Remarks and references to Appendices.
8th June VLAMERTINGHE	29th Lancers move from Brickfields Ehuts	
9th – 11th June "	No change	
12th June VLAMERTINGHE	VLAMERTINGHE and camp shelled intermittently from 6 p.m. to 9 p.m. VLAMERTINGHE church burnt. Bde. HQrs. Details employed in burning ammunition & trenches and in extinguishing fire which broke out in house close to church.	
13th June "	Camps shelled in early morning. No casualties in Bde. G.O.C. 2d. Cav.Dn. ordering Bde. to retire to billeting area on 14th. received.	
14th June L'ERKELSBRUGGE	Bde. entrained 7 a.m. and reaches billeting area 10 a.m. 1st Ind. Cav.Dn. onto No 10 area.	
15th June MAMETZ	Bde. billeting in Billet R.H.A. marches 8.15 am & reaches MAMETZ area 1.30 p.m. Batts & units in same billets as previous march.	
16th June MAMETZ	Bde. at 4 hours notice to move.	

WAR DIARY

June 1915

Army Form C. 2118.

LUCKNOW Cavalry Brigade

Intelligence Summary

(Erase heading not required.)

Hour, Date, Place.	Summary of Events and Information.	Remarks and references to Appendices.
17 – 27 June	No change	
28 June	Capt. Muspratt XII Cav. B.M. left the Bde. as GSO 2. 2nd Cav Bde.	D.W: A 1326 27.6.15
	Capt. Maitland 14' Jat Lancers assumed duties of Bde Major.	
	- McLeod - Guides Cav " " " Staff Captain.	
29-30 June	No change	

A.R.Maitland
Capt. B.M.

Serial No. 111.

121/6502

WAR DIARY
OF
Lucknow Cavalry Brigade.

FROM 1st July 1915 TO 31st July 1915

WAR DIARY
or
INTELLIGENCE SUMMARY

Army Form C. 2118.

Inclosure. Car Brigade Section ending July 31st 1915.

Hour, Date, Place	Summary of Events and Information	Remarks and references to Appendices
1st July 1915 MAMETZ	No change. Routine work average of messages received 65/ per month.	
2nd July 1915 "	Camp for 2nd class	
3. "	Routine work. Buzzer kit, saddle & rifle inspection	
	Buzzer & swimming parade	
4 July 1915	Went on staff ride to discuss the signalling part	
5 "	Buzzer	
6 "	Helio and flag	
7 "	Buzzer	
8 "	Laying telephone wire & practicing with commutator	
9 "	Buzzer	
10 "	Camp	
11 "	Flag	
12 "	Helio	grazing	
13 "	Staff ride with regimental signallers	
14 "	Camp with regimental signallers	
	Grazing & horse inspection	

Army Form C. 2118.

WAR DIARY
or
INTELLIGENCE SUMMARY
(Erase heading not required.)

Lucknow Cav Bde
ending July 31/1915

Hour, Date, Place	Summary of Events and Information	Remarks and references to Appendices
15 July 1915	No change Routine work - Officers class of ly starter	
16	" buzzer - practice	
17	" helio 9 flag	
18	" air line practise in layout	
19	" camp	
20	" Staff ride with regtal sigs	
21	" buzzer hel in speeches	
22	" helio	
23	" paging	
24	" camp	
25	" helio	
26	" buzzer graphing	
27	" buzzer	
28	" kit inspection	
29		
30		

Kenneth Hoare
Capt
O.C. Signal Troop

Serial No. 111.

Confidential

121/7286

War Diary

with Appendices

of

Lucknow Cavalry Brigade.

FROM 1st August 1915, TO 13th September 21st August 1915.

August 1915   Cavalry Brigade now   Army Form C. 2118.

WAR DIARY
INTELLIGENCE SUMMARY
(Erase heading not required.)

Hour, Date, Place.	Summary of Events and Information.	Remarks and references to Appendices.

2nd FRUGES —

3rd MARESQUEL.

28.

August 1st

Brigade marched to new billeting area for attachment to 3rd Cavy. H.Q. 1st Ind Cav. R.H.A Bde. U Battery R.H.A, Divnl Ammn. Col. 21(I) Squadron R.E. Lucknow Field Amb & Corps Remount Section were attached to Brigade during the move. Bde. went into billets. HQ. R.H.A. FRUGES — R.H.A. Batty. FRUGES — K.D.G. MATRINGHAM 29th SENLIS. 38th FRUGES — Divnl troops LUGY & HEZECQUES.

Brigade marched in 3 columns; Bde. hrs A echelon under Brigadier. R.H.A, Field Squadron + A echelon under O.C. R.H.A. Bde. B echelon — Field Amb — Mot. Pak + Remount See under O.C. A.S.C. went into billets — Hqr — K.D.G MARESQUEL — 29th CONTES 38th ESQUEMICOURT — R.H.A? Divnl troops AUBAIN - ST VAAST.

The Brigade again marched in 3 columns to a billeting area S. of the ABBEVILLE — BERNAVILLE road turning out as follows:— H.Q. HOUDENCOURT — K.D.G DOMQUEUR — 29th FRANSU — 38th RIBEAUCOURT. U Battery BEAUMETZ — Ammn Col. LONGVILLERS — Field Squadron R.E MESNIL — Field Amb. Remount Sec. LES MASSURES — Hq. R.H.A + A.S.C
MAISON ROLLAND

Ainsworth
Brigade Major

Army Form C. 2118.

WAR DIARY
or
INTELLIGENCE SUMMARY
Lucknow Cavalry Brigade

(Erase heading not required.)

Instructions regarding War Diaries and Intelligence Summaries are contained in F.S. Regs., Part II, and the Staff Manual respectively. Title pages will be prepared in manuscript.

Hour, Date, Place.	Summary of Events and Information.	Remarks and references to Appendices.
August 4th HOUDEN COURT	Divisional troops have moved into their new area by Divisions. The Brigade marched into billets as follows:— Brig. H.Q. BERTHEAUCOURT, K.D.G. & 29th ST LEGER — 36th BERTHEAUCOURT	
" 7th BERTHEAUCOURT	A larger area having been allotted to the Brigade, the H.Q. moved into CANAPLES the 29th into MONTRELET & FIEFFES — The K.D.G's into PERNOIS and HALLOY — The whole of BERTHEAUCOURT was allotted to the 36th	
" 22nd CANAPLES	In accordance with O.O. attached the Brigade French party marched under Lt.Col. Roome 36th F.J.H. & embarked on night 22/23rd in W and E.N.E. of FORCEVILLE, the ladies horses returning to BEAUCOURT thence to permanent billets on night 23/24th	See app. O.O.
23rd FORCEVILLE	The Brigade marched at 5.p.m. via MARTINSART & AUTHUILLE & relieved the MHOW Brigade in Reserve. The relief was completed at 12 m.n.	
"24th – Aug 3rd AUTHUILLE	The Brigade held AUTHUILLE as follows — 1 Sqdn K.D.G's & M.G.s K.D.G. 3 Sqdn Sql. MACMAHON'S POST — 1 Sqdn 29 F.L. GORDON CASTLE 3 Sqdns K.D.G 2 Sqdn Sql. 4 Sqdns 36th F.J.H. AUTHUILLE. The whole of our work is finding AUTHUILLE in particular a state[?]	Our Gunners have been Brig Maj

Army Form O. 2118.

WAR DIARY
or
INTELLIGENCE SUMMARY.
(Erase heading not required.)

Instructions regarding War Diaries and Intelligence Summaries are contained in F. S. Regs., Part II, and the Staff Manual respectively. Title pages will be prepared in manuscript.

Hour, Date, Place.	Summary of Events and Information.	Remarks and references to Appendices.
Aug. 28th CANAPLES.	Of defence on the 25th. Lt Col Saunders 29 F.L returned to Col. Rome in command of the French party. Lt Col Bell Smyth took over command at 29 F.L until the Brigade was relieved. The Casualties during this time were K.D.G. Wounded O.R.2. 29 F.L Wounded 1 O.R. 38 F.L killed 1.O.S.1. 1.O.R. 1. Wounded 1.O.R. 2. Brigade Hd moved to BERNEVIC.	
Sept 2nd AUTHUILLE	The Brigade was relieved by Scendentant in accordance with O.3. relief being completed at 11.0 a.m. Whilst Horses of Brigade met the front party at PICQUIGNY moved 9 carts moved independently to billeting area at BEAUCOURT arriving about 7.0 a.m.	App. O.3.
3rd BEAUCOURT	Brigade found a digging party of 300 men for 3rd line trenches near SENLIS	
6th ,,	Digging party returned to billets leaving out 111 diggers 9 L. horseholders	
12th AUTHUILLE	1st Indian Cavalry Div relieved 2nd Ind. Cav Div ??? under Brig Gen E Parker to the trenches Meerut Division "Sackson" Brigade relieved Lucendentant in reserve in AUTHUILLE a night of 12/13	

AnBurrowby
Brig Gen

Secret.

Lucknow Bde

Copy No. 7 O.2

1st INDIAN CAVALRY DIVISIONAL OPERATION ORDER NO. 12.

20th August 1915.

Reference Map 1/20,000

1.   The Division will occupy and hold the trenches between AUTHUILLE and HAMEL known as "F" Sector of 51st Division.
       The Sector will be divided into two sub-sectors as follows :-

F-1. To be held by Ambala Brigade relieving Meerut Brigade. From a point about 70 yards South of AUTHUILLE - OVILLERS Road where the sector adjoins next Brigade (E Sector) to the point where the line ends the South curve of the circular drive West of the CHATEAU of THIEPVAL.

F-2. To be held by Sialkot Brigade relieving Secunderabad Brigade. From the last mentioned point to the River ANCRE where the sector joins and overlaps that held by the next brigade (G Sector).

Lucknow Brigade will occupy AUTHUILLE.

2.   Sub-sectors F-1, F-2 and AUTHUILLE will each be commanded by a regimental commandant selected by the Brigadiers.
       These two subsectors and AUTHUILLE will be commanded by Brigadier General Leader with his brigade staff. His normal headquarters will be in AUTHUILLE but in case of attack the Command Post will be the railway bridge North West of AUTHUILLE known as PONT D'AUTHUILLE.

3.   Brigades and Divisional Troops will move as in the attached accompanying March Table.
       The Divisional Troops will be under the command of the Officer Commanding Field Squadron, R.E.

4.   Strength of Brigades - 900 rifles.
       Only 3/5ths of officers will be taken.

5.   An Advanced Dressing Station will be opened at AUTHUILLE.
       One Cavalry Field Ambulance will be situated at CONTAY.

6.   The Advanced Report Centre will open in the wood East North East of FORCEVILLE at 1.0 p.m., on 22nd

C.A.C. Godwin
Lieutenant Colonel,
General Staff,
1st Indian Cavalry Division.

Issued at 2 pm.

O.2

SECRET. Operation Order No. 7 Copy No. 7
by
~~MQQQQ~~ Brig-General W.H.FASKEN, Comdg Lucknow Cav Bde.

Reference 1/20,000 and AMIENS 1/20,000 Maps.   20th August 1915.

1.   The Division will occupy and hold the trenches between AUTHUILLE and HAMEL known as "F" Sector of 51st Division.
        The Sector will be divided into two sub-sectors as follows:-

F-1. To be held by Ambala Brigade relieving Meerut Brigade From a point about 70 yards South of AUTHUILLE-OVILLERS road where the Sector adjoins next Brigade (E Sector) to the point where the line ends the South curve of the circular drive West of the CHATEAU of THIEPVAL.

F-2. To be held by Sialkot Brigade relieving Secunderabad Brigade. From the last mentioned point to the River ANCRE where the Sector joins and overlaps that held by the next Brigade (C Sector).

        LUCKNOW Brigade will occupy AUTHUILLE.

                                                        each
2.   Sub-sectors F-1, F-2 and AUTHUILLE will be commanded by a regimental commandant selected by the Brigadiers.
        These two sub-sectors and AUTHUILLE will be commanded by Brigadier General LEADER with his brigade staff. His normal headquarters will be in AUTHUILLE but in case of attack the Command Post will be the railway bridge North West of AUTHUILLE known as PONT D'AUTHUILLE.

3.   The Brigade will march at 4-0 p.m. on 22nd instant, via WARGNIES-TALMAS-RUBEMPRE-BEAUCOURT-WARLOY to road junction 500 yards East of last E of FORCEVILLE.
        Starting Point WARGNIES CHURCH 4-0 p.m.
        Order of March.
            Advanced Guard   1 Sqdn 29th Lancers
            Main Body   Brigade Signal Troop
                               29th Lancers (less 1 Sqdn)
                               King's Dragoon Guards
                               36th Jacob's Horse
        The Brigade will halt for 1½ hours to water and feed at BEAUCOURT.

4.   A Echelon and the 2 G.S.Wagons per Regt, each carrying 10 dismounted men will march in the above order from the same starting point at 3-0 p.m., under Lieut FOX, K.D.Gds.
        Route as above.
        They will water and feed at EBART Fm.

5.   With reference to para 4 Divisional Instructions attached, O.C. K.D.Gds will detail one officer to report to the A.Q.M.G. at Divnl Headquarters at 8-30 a.m. 22nd instant.

6.   When the whole Division has arrived in bivouac the led horses of both Brigades will then move off to BEAUCOURT via route they came, AMBALA Brigade leading.
        Lt-Col J.A.Bell-Smyth, K.D.Gds will be in charge of the Brigade led horses.

7.	Quartermasters of Units and 26 men per Regt will parade at Brigade Headquarters at 7-45 a.m. 22nd instant, and proceed by lorry to FORCEVILLE in accordance with paras 2, 16 and 17.

8.	Regtl Ammunition reserve will not be taken, instructions regarding transport will issue later.

9.	The following medical personnel will accompany the Brigade:-
    Capt J.F.James, I.M.S.
    1 Sub-Assistant Surgeon, 36th J.Horse.
    1 Medical Orderly, K.D.Gds.

10.	The Advanced Brigade Report Centre will open in Wood E.N.E. of FORCEVILLE at 11-0 p.m.

                                          [signature] Major.
                        Brigade Major, Lucknow Cavalry Brigade.

Copy No. 1 6 KDG
        2 29 L
        3 36 JH.
        4 Sigs
        5 Supply Off.
        6 Capt James I.M.S.
        7 Retained.

Copy No. 7

1st INDIAN CAVALRY DIVISION OPERATION ORDER NO. 14.

31st August 1915.

The Division will be relieved by the 2nd Indian Cavalry Division on the night of 2nd/3rd September under arrangements similar to the relief on the night of the 23rd/24th August 1915.

Advance officers will arrive to take over trenches as before.

Ambala Brigade will be relieved by Mhow Brigade. Sialkot Brigade by Meerut Brigade. Lucknow Brigade by Secunderabad Brigade.

2. The Meerut Brigade should leave Road junction 500 yards East of last E of FORCEVILLE at 7.45 p.m., on 2nd September. At MARTINSART it will be met by 12 guides one per squadron from Sialkot Brigade. Mhow Brigade will follow and will be met by guides from Ambala Brigade. Secunderabad Brigade will follow Mhow Brigade and be met by guides from Lucknow Brigade. These guides will report at Headquarters, MARTINSART at 8.0 p.m., on 2nd September and be provided with a paper stating who they are. Sub-sectors will be relieved from left to right.

3. On arrival at MARTINSART, Brigades of 1st Indian Cavalry Division will load their kits on their transport and march to where the horses are formed up at Road junction 500 yards East of last E of FORCEVILLE. Order of march.

    Lucknow Brigade to leave MARTINSART as soon as transport is loaded.
    Ambala Brigade.
    Sialkot Brigade.

Billeting areas are -
    Advanced Report Centre - MONTIGNY.
    Lucknow Brigade ST GRATIEN. FRECHEN Court
    Sialkot Brigade - BEAUCOURT.
    Ambala Brigade - MONTIGNY.

5. 1st Field Squadron, R.E., on relief will move to BEAUCOURT.

6. The Signal Squadron on relief will move to MONTIGNY.

7. Medical units at AUTHUILLE on relief will move to MONTIGNY.

8. Transport of Brigades, in order of march of Brigades will be formed up at MARTINSART by 11.0 a.m., As Brigades arrive wagons will be loaded and when complete will march off in rear of their brigades.

9. Advanced Report Centre will close at MARTINSART at 4.0 a.m., 3rd September and open at MONTIGNY same hour.

C.A.C. Godwin
Lieutenant Colonel,
General Staff,
1st Indian Cavalry Division.

Copy No. 1 G.S., Indian Cavalry Corps.
2 2nd Indian Cavalry Division.
3 51st (Highland) Division.
4 "G" Sector.
5 Sialkot Brigade.
6 Ambala Brigade.
7 Lucknow Brigade.
8 A.D.M.S.,
9 A.D.V.S.,
10 S.R.E.O
11 O.C., A.S.C.,
12 O.C. Divisional Signal Squadron.
13 Supply Officer, Advanced Troops.
14-18 File, diary and office.

Operation Order No. 8 Copy No.
by Brig-General W.H.Fasken,
Commanding Lucknow Cavalry Brigade.

Reference AMIENS 1/80,000 Map. 1-9-15.

1. The Trench Party will be relieved by the SECUNDERABAD Brigade on the night of 2nd/3rd September and move to billeting area ST GRATIEN - FRECHENCOURT.

2. A led horse party (Major Meynell 29th Lrs Comdg) will be despatched from permanent billets to meet the Trench Party at the road junction East of the last E of FORCEVILLE and convey it to billeting area ST GRATIEN - FRECHENCOURT.

The led horse party will consist of mounted men leading 2 horses each. An officer will be in charge of each regimental party.
A lorry will be provided at the road junction to carry 20 men of the K.D.Gds to save personnel of horse conducting parties. The men thus carried will be taken to permanent billets.

Starting Point for led horses Road Junction East end of WARGNIES at 4 p.m. on 2nd September.

Order of March ... 29th Lrs.
K.D.Gds.
36th J.H.

Route - TALMAS-HERISSART-TOUTENCOURT-HARPONVILLE-VARENNES thence via HEDAUVILLE to the road junction East of last E of FORCEVILLE arriving there at 9 p.m.

Horses will be watered on the road at point to be notified later, and will be fed on arrival at FORCEVILLE.

3. The Officer in charge of led horses of K.D.Gds will meet a Divisional Staff Officer at the road junction East of the last E of FORCEVILLE at 8 p.m. on 2nd September 1915, to find out the forming up place for the led horse party.

4. A billeting party consisting of 1 man per squadron under an officer 36th Jacob's Horse will meet a Divisional Staff Officer at BEAUCOURT CHURCH at 10 a.m. 2nd September.

These men will be transported in lorries from permanent billets under arrangements to be notified later.

These parties will be responsible for meeting and guiding units to their billets on arrival from the trenches.

5. B Echelon will accompany the led horse party
    Capt. H. Crawford P.L.Gds.   Commanding.
In order of march of led horse parties.
Starting point road junction E end of WARGNIES at 5-15 p.m.
Route - TALMAS-PIERREGOT-MOLLIENS AU BOIS-St GRATIEN.
Not to arrive at MOLLIENS au BOIS till 7-30 p.m.
Destination St GRATIEN and FRECHENCOURT.

6. Led horse parties will return to permanent billets on 3rd September
7. The Bde Veterinary Officer will accompany the party.
8. Details as to what is to be carried on B Echelon will be communicated later.

Issued at 9 a.m.

D.McLeod. Captain.
for Brigade Major, Lucknow Cavalry Brigade.

& conducting parties

INSTRUCTIONS FOR LED HORSE PARTY.

Each Brigade will despatch from its permanent billeting area a led horse party to convey the relieved trench party from the road junction East of the last E of FORCEVILLE, to its billeting area about BEAUCOURT SUR L'HALLUE.

The led horse party of each Brigade will be accompanied by its "B" Echelon and will march as in the accompanying march table..

2. Each Brigade led-horse party will consist of 150 mounted men leading 300 horses per regiment.

An officer will be in charge of each Brigade party. Brigade Veterinary Officers will accompany the parties. Lorries will be provided at the road junction for each British regiment to carry 20 men each to save personnel of horse conducting parties. The men thus carried will be taken straight back to permanent billets.

3. Brigades will detail a billeting party (one man per squadron) to meet a Divisional Staff Officer at BEAUCOURT Church at 10.0 a.m., 2nd September. The A.Q.M.G. will arrange the transport of these men in two lorries from billets. These parties will be responsible for meeting and guiding units to their billets on arrival from the trenches.

4. A Divisional Staff Officer will meet representatives of the led-horse party of each brigade at the road junction East of the last E of FORCEVILLE at 8.0 p.m., tp show them the forming up places for brigade parties.

SECRET. Copy of ADMINISTRATIVE INSTRUCTIONS No. G-3307 dated 1st September 1915., from 1st Indian Cavalry Division.

Reference G-3298. Previous Instructions.

INSTRUCTIONS FOR LED HORSE PARTY.

1. Reference G-298. B Echelon. Not more than one G.S. Wagon per unit will go to the BEAUCOURT area.

2. Two Lorries for each British regiment will be provided, each carrying 20 men. The corresponding less number of led horses will be taken.

3. One Lorry per Brigade will call for Billeting Parties as follows:-

    AMBALA Brigade   7 - 0 a.m.   X roads in L'ETOILE.
    SIALKOT Brigade   7-15 a.m.   The Church St OUEN.
    LUCKNOW Brigade   7-30 a.m.   Railway Bridge CANAPLES.

One British or Indian Officer for each Unit will accompany the Billeting Parties.

4. Supplies for 3rd September will be taken over at 5-0 p.m. on the 2nd by the billeting parties in the BEAUCOURT area.

Half grain and fodder only will be issued in the BEAUCOURT area for the led horse party; the remainder will be issued in permanent billets to await their return.

5. Indents for Ordnance Stores required to be delivered in the BEAUCOURT area should be marked "Digging Party". All other stores will be delivered in the permanent billeting area.

No. S.C.542.   1st September 1915.

Forwarded for information and necessary action, in continuation of pervious instructions.

                                                        Captain.
                                    for Staff Captain, Lucknow Cavalry Bde.

To The ....

MOVEMENT TABLE FOR LED HORSE PARTY, 1st Ind. Cav. Divn.

Unit.	Route, &c. on Sept 2nd
Lucknow Bde led horse party. *16¼ miles from Wargnies Church*	Route from permanent billets. TALMAS, HERISSART, TOUTENCOURT, HARPONVILLE VARENNES, thence via HEDAUVILLE to the road junction East of the last E of FORCEVILLE, arriving there at 9.0 p.m.,
"B" Echelon LUCKNOE Bde. *9¼ miles Molliens au bois 7.¼*	TALMAS, PIERREGOT, MOLLIENS-AU-BOIS, ST GRATIEN (Not to arrive at MOLLIENS-AU-BOIS till 7.30 p.m., Destination. ST GRATIEN and FRECHENCOURT.
Sialkot Bde Led horse party.	VIGNACOURT, FLESSELLES, VILLERS BOCAGE, MOLLIENS-AU-BOIS, BEAUCOURT, WARLOY. (To be clear of MOLLIENS-AU-BOIS by 6.30 p.m.,) Destination Road junction East of last E of FORCEVILLE, arriving there at 9.30 p.m.,
"B" Echelon Sialkot Bde.	Same route as led horse party to BEAUCOURT, SUR L'HALLUE (To be clear of MOLLIENS-AU-BOIS by 6.30 p.m., Destination BEAUCOURT SUR L'HALLUE, arriving there at 9.30 p.m.,
Ambala Bde led horse party.	VIGNACOURT, FLESSELLES, VILLERS BOCAGE, MOLLIENS-AU-BOIS, BEAUCOURT, SUR L'HALLUE, WARLOY. (To be clear of MOLLIENS-AU-BOIS by 7.0 p.m.,) Destination, Road junction east of last E of FORCEVILLE at 10.0 p.m.,
"B" Echelon Ambala Bde.	Same route as led horse party to MOLLIENS-AU-BOIS then MONTIGNY (To be clear of MOLLIENS-AU-BOIS by 7.0 p.m.,) Destination MONTIGNY, arriving there at 10.0 p.m.,

Led Horse parties move by routes by which they came to permanent billets, on Sept 3rd

12/17601

Serial No. 111.

Confidential
War Diary
with appendices.

of

Lucknow Cavalry Brigade.

FROM 13th September 1915 TO 31st September October 1915

Army Form C. 2118.

WAR DIARY
or
INTELLIGENCE SUMMARY.
(Erase heading not required.)

Instructions regarding War Diaries and Intelligence Summaries are contained in F. S. Regs., Part II, and the Staff Manual respectively. Title pages will be prepared in manuscript.

25 NOV 1915

Hour, Date, Place.	Summary of Events and Information.	Remarks and references to Appendices.
AUTHUILLE Sept 14th	On the night of 14/11/15 the Lucknow Brigade relieved the Cumbs La Brigade in G.1 Subsector. York and Front line Trenches, K.D.G.s in right, 29th in centre, 28th in left. The casualties during this tour of duty were :- K.D.G.s 1 wounded, 29th 3 killed 14 wounded, 38th 5 wounded.	
AUTHUILLE Sept. 16th	On the night of the 16/17th the Division was relieved by the 14th and 16th Bdes. The relief was completed at 11 p.m. The Brigade marched by squadrons to PERCEVILLE Wood where the led horse party were waiting. Thence Brigade proceeded to billets around BEAUCOURT.	
BEAUCOURT 17th	Brigade marched at 8 a.m. to permanent billeting area, Bde H.Q. having previously moved to ST LEGER.	
ST LEGER 21st	The Indian Cavalry Corps was inspected by Field Marshal Lord Kitchener near SORCAMPS.	
" 22nd	Brigade marched at 2 p.m. to a position of readiness WJ DOULLENS & went into billets as follows: Bgde HQ MON PLAISIR - KDGs AUTHEUX - 29th HARDINVAL & CONCHES - 38th LONGUEVILLETTE - First Vet Sec. LE QUESNEL Fm	0.6.
MON PLAISIR 25th	Brigade was put at 2½ hours notice to move to later on 1 hr notice. All R.Gs were dumped in local buildings. T.G.S. wagon loads loaded, and at 2 days corn ration Pack Animals were loaded with another two days After loading up, in DOULLENS G.S. wagons & pack returned Brigade	

signature Brigade Major

Army Form C. 2118.

WAR DIARY
INTELLIGENCE SUMMARY.
(Erase heading not required.)

[Stamp: LUCKNOW CAVALRY BRIGADE]

Instructions regarding War Diaries and Intelligence Summaries are contained in F. S. Regs., Part II, and the Staff Manual respectively. Title pages will be prepared in manuscript.

Hour, Date, Place.		Summary of Events and Information.	Remarks and references to Appendices.
MON PLAISIR. Oct 3rd		Brigade put on 4 hours notice to move.	
"	10th	" " " " " "	
"	13th	K.T.G. & 3d S. moved into billets in BERNAVILLE. "U" Battery rejoined Brigade from billets in AUTHEUX with 1 Squadron	
"	29th		
"	22nd	Brigade marched, in accordance with attd orders, to winter billeting area from billets in for them. Bde Hq CAVILLON	O.7
		"U" Battery FOURDRINOY – K.T.G MOLLIENSVIDAMS and CAMPS (HQ)	
		24th PICQUIGNY & ST PIERRE-A-GOUY – 36th V.H. LE MES GIS RIENCOURT OISSY (HQ) – CAV. Field Amb. PICQUIGNY –	
		Mob Vet. CAVILLON.	
CAVILLON "	31st	No change.	

Lieutenant Colonel
Brigade Major

Secret

Copy No. 11

O.4.

LUCKNOW CAVALRY BRIGADE OPERATION ORDER No. 9

Reference AMIENS Map. 1/20,000.   10th Sept 1915.

1. The Division will relieve 2nd Indian Cav Div in the trenches on the night of 12/13th September, under arrangements similar to the relief on 2/3rd September.
   G 1 Sector will be held by AMBALA Brigade, and G 2 by SIALKOT Brigade. LUCKNOW Brigade will be in support at AUTHUILLE.

2. Officers will go up in advance as before, reporting at MARTINSART at 6-0 p.m. 11th instant, and will send their horses back to ST GRATIEN area.

3. The G.O.C will be in command of the Cavalry Sector with headquarters at MARTINSART.
   Lt Col SAUNDERS will command LUCKNOW dismounted Brigade.

4. Strength of regiments will be 220 rifles in the trenches, and 3/5 of the number of officers in proper proportion of ranks.

5. The Brigade will march at 8-0 p.m. on 11th instant, to the area ST GRATIEN-FRECHENCOURT via TALMAS-PIERREGOT-MOLLIENS au BOIS. Starting Point X roads at East end of WARGNIES.
   Order of march - Advance Guard   1 sqdn K.D.Gds.
                   Main Body   Bde Signal Troop
                                  King's Dragoon Guards (less 1 squadron).
                                  36th Jacob's Horse.
                                  29th Lancers.

6. Transport will march in order of units in rear of the brigade under Lieut FOX, K.D.Gds.

7. On arrival at ST GRATIEN the brigade will move into same billets as occupied before by Digging Party.

8. The brigade will march from ST GRATIEN area to MARTINSART on evening of 12th September, under orders to be issued by Lt Col SAUNDERS.

9. Lt Col BELL-SMYTH will command the brigade on the march to ST GRATIEN tomorrow evening, and will be in command of the led horses returning from MARTINSART on night of 12/13th.
   A selected officer will be placed in charge of the led horse party of each unit.

10. Orders for medical personnel and equipment will be issued by Captain A.C.MUNRO, I.M.S.

11. The Advanced Brigade Report Centre will open at FRECHENCOURT at 10-30 p.m. on 11th instant.

Issued at 4-30 p.m.

DM Leod.
Captain.
for Brigade Major, Lucknow Cavalry Brigade.

No. Copies
1 - KDG   5 - Supply Offr   10 } Retained.
2 - 29 L   6 - Sept Offr   11 }
3 - 36 JH   7 - Capt Munro IMS
4 - Sigs   8 - Lt Col Saunders
           9 - KDG

Secret

INSTRUCTIONS TO ACCOMPANY DIVISIONAL OPERATION ORDER No.16.

1. On arrival at BEAUCOURT area Brigades will move into same billets as they were before.

2. Representatives of units will meet Divisional Staff Officer at 5 p.m. 12th at West entrance of MARTINSART where they will be shown the places fixed for dismounting.

3. Led horses of the Division will march back to BEAUCOURT under orders of the senior officer of the parties. From BEAUCOURT Brigade led horse parties will proceed to permanent billets via routes they came.

4. Brigades will go into trenches in the following order:-
   Sialkot Brigade
   Ambala Brigade
   Lucknow Brigade.
Officers commanding brigades will find out from units they are relieving, order of relief and communicate the same to their brigades.

5. 40 dismounted men per British regiment will leave regimental headquarters at 2-0 p.m. Sunday, 12th and proceed in lorries to "point 97" East of FORCEVILLE where they will dismount and proceed on foot to MARTINSART at 7-0 p.m. and await arrival of the mounted troops from BEAUCOURT area.

6. Troops will take their greatcoats in addition to waterproof sheets and blankets.

7. With the exception of two G.S wagons, one cook cart and one water cart per unit, only pack transport will accompany troops.
G.S wagons will convey blankets and waterproof sheets as far as MARTINSART where they will remain packed night of 12/13th and be unpacked and conveyed to trenches next day under brigade arrangements.

8. Pack transport will accompany each squadron from BEAUCOURT area to prevent any delay at MARTINSART, where troops will dismount and march straight into trenches.

9. Advanced officers will take over carefully all trench stores and ammunition, as many discrepancies occurred in last relief.

10. Ambala Cavalry Field Ambulance will move to CONTAY and Advanced Dressing Station from BEAUCOURT will move to AUTHUILLE.

11. All other details as in last relief.

SECRET.

Major James   O.5.

Copy No. 7

LUCKNOW BRIGADE OPERATION ORDER No. 10.

Reference AMIENS Map 1/80,000.   14th September 1915.

1. The 1st Indian Cavalry Division will be relieved in the trenches on the night of 16th/17th September by the 51st Highland Division.

2. The led horse party (Major GREEN 36th J.Horse Commanding) will march at 1-0 p.m. on 16th instant to the area St GRATIEN FRECHENCOURT, via TALMAS-PIERREGOT.
     Starting Point - X roads at East end of WARGNIES.

     Order of March :   Signal Troop,
                         King's Dragoon Guards,
                         36th Jacob's Horse,
                         29th Lancers.

3. On arrival at St GRATIEN area units will water and put down lines and will march again at 7-40 p.m. to the forming up ground ¼ mile N.E. of last E of FORCEVILLE, via CONTAY-WARLOYBAILLON-MAILLY road.
     Brigade starting point - Cross roads at first E of FRECHENCOURT
     Order of march   Brigade Signal Troop
                             29th Lancers
                             36th Jacob's Horse
                             King's Dragoon Guards.

4. After picking up trench party at Divisional forming up ground Brigades will move back to St GRATIEN and FRECHENCOURT by the same route as mentioned above and will go into billets.

5. The Brigade will return from St GRATIEN area to permanent billets by the same route as mentioned in para 1, at 6-0 p.m. on 17th instant, under orders of Lt Col SAUNDERS.

6. A British Officer will be in charge of led horses of each unit.

                                         D McLeod.
                                                     Captain.
       for Bde Major, Lucknow Cavalry Brigade.

DIVISIONAL TABLE OF LED HORSE PARTIES.

16th SEPTEMBER.

    LUCKNOW BRIGADE   via TALMAS PIERREGOT to ST GRATIEN and
                             FRECHENCOURT. The party to be clear of the
                             cross roads ½ mile North West of ½ mile North West
                             of ST GRATIEN by 3-0 p.m. To water at ST GRATIEN
                             and FRECHENCOURT.

For the march from BEAUCOURT area to the forming up ground.

BEAUCOURT Church will be the Divisional Starting Point.

Sialkot Brigade with Jodhpur Lancers attached.	Under command of Major Battye, 6th Cavalry.
Ambala Brigade.	In order named will pass BEAUCOURT
Lucknow Brigade.	Church at 7-30 p.m., 8-0 p.m. and 8-20 p.m. respectively and move to forming up ground ½ mile North East of last E of PORCEVILLE, which will be reached at 10-0 p.m.

Night of 16/17th September.

On arrival of trench parties, Brigades will mount and move to BEAUCOURT area via main CONTAY road. Rear to be clear of WARLOY BAILLON by 4-30 a.m. 17th September.

"A" Form.
MESSAGES AND SIGNALS.

Army Form C. 2121.

Prefix	Code	m.	Words	Charge	This message is on a/c of:	Recd. at	r.i.
Office of Origin and Service Instructions			Sent		Service.	Date	
			At	m.		From	
			To				
			By		(Signature of "Franking Officer.")	By	

TO { OC KRG
      2y⁹
      38

Sender's Number	Day of Month	In reply to Number	
*BM 309	22		AAA

1. The Bde will march at 2.0 pm starting point N end of MONTRELET head on FIENVILLERS road. Order of march 13 Bg⁴ (adv⁰ ⓖ 1.30 pm)
   KRG⁴
   38ᵗʰ
   (Bn Transp A) A echelon in rear of unit
                  B

2. Motor cycle will meet the Staff Captain at the crossroads junction at Mesin.

3. Units will billet in villages as follows:-
   KRG⁴ AUTHEUX & 31ᵗʰ LONGVILLERS
   29ᵗʰ GORGES HARBINCAU

4. Bde HQ MON PLAISIR

5. Bde report centre will close at 2.0 pm open at MON PLAISIR as ½ an hour

From
Place
Time

The above may be forwarded as now corrected. (Z)
Censor.   Signature of Addressor or person authorised to telegraph in his name.

* This line should be erased if not required.

(15491) S. & Co. Ltd. W 14142/641. 90,000. 4/15. Forms C 2121/18.

"A" Form. Army Form C. 2121.

MESSAGES AND SIGNALS.

No. of Message 1

Prefix — Code MEA m. Words 36 Charge — | This message is on a/c of: | Recd. at 12.55 m. Date 23.1x
Office of Origin and Service Instructions
VIA
Priority

Sent At ___ m. To ___ By ___

Service.

From VIA
By Crawford

TO **Lucknow Bde**

Sender's Number: GA 357
Day of Month: 21
In reply to Number:
A A A

Field day cancelled for tomorrow aaa division will move to new billeting area leaving present billets about noon aaa Detailed orders follow in the morning.

From / Place / Time: 1st Ind Cav Div 11.3 pm

The above may be forwarded as now corrected. (Z)

Censor. Signature of Addressee or person authorised to telegraph in his name
* This line should be erased if not required.
(15491) S. & Co. Ltd. W 14142/641. 90,000. 4/15. Forms C 2121/10.

SECRET

Copy No. 5

1st INDIAN CAVALRY DIVISION OPERATION ORDER NO. 19.

22nd September 1915.

Reference Map 80,000

1. 1st Indian Cavalry Division will move to a new billeting area today in accordance with accompanying March Table.

2. Troops (and Transport) will be north of the line BEAUMETZ – LONGUE VILLETTE by 3.30 p.m.

3. Billeting officers of Divisional Troops will meet A.A., and Q.M.G., at Divisional Headquarters DOMART at 10.0 a.m. They will be prepared to ride on at once to arrange billets for their units.

4. Divisional Troops under orders of Lieut: Colonel Rouse, D.S.O., R.H.A., will march as follows :-
Starting point Cross roads 200 yards south of ES of LANCHES at 1.0 p.m.

Order of march.
    R.H.A., Brigade,............1.0 p.m.
    Field Squadron, R.E.......1.20 p.m.,
    Divisional Headquarters...
    Cavalry Field Ambulances..NOTE–The Lucknow Cavalry Field
                                  Ambulance will join the Column at
                                  BERNAVILLE.
    "B" Echelon of units in
    order of march,...........1.35.0.p.m.,

5. Report Centre will remain at DOMART till 3.30 p.m. New Report Centre will be communicated later.

C.A.L. Godwin Lt.Col:
General Staff,
1st Indian Cavalry Division.

Issued at 5.0 a.m., by D.R.

No. 1	to Indian Cavalry Corps.	No. 7	to A.D.V.S.,
2	2nd Indian Cavalry Division.	8	O.C. A.S.C.,
3	Sialkot Brigade	9	Senior Supply Off:
4	Mhow Brigade.	10	Field Squadron.
5	Lucknow Brigade.	11	Signal Squadron.
6	A.D.M.S.	12	Camp Commdt.
		13	Liaison Officer.
		14 – 17	File, diary &c.

Secret

No. G-331.

Headquarters,
1st Indian Cavalry Division.
20th October 1915.

O.7

MEMORANDUM.

The Division will move to new billeting area on October 22nd as under :-

Mhow Brigade.	Via DOMART – LA FOLIE AUBERGE cross roads – ETOILE – CONDE FOLIE – QUESNOY. No portion of the Brigade to be East of or on BERNAVILLE – BERNEUIL Road after 8.30 a.m. and whole brigade to be clear of CONDE FOLIE by 12.30 p.m.
Lucknow Brigade	Via FIENVILLERS – MONTRELET – CANAPLES – VIGNACOURT – PICQUIGNY. To be clear of BERNAVILLE by 8.30 a.m.
Sialkot Brigade	Via BERNAVILLE – BERNEUIL – PERNOIS – ST OUEN – FLIXECOURT – HANGEST SUR SOMME and not to enter BERNAVILLE till 8.30 a.m.
Divl Headquarters	Will follow Mhow Brigade.
Ammunition Column Field Squadron One field Ambulance from DOMART.	In order named under Officer Commanding Field Squadron. Via CONDE FOLIE – QUESNOY – METIGNY and to be clear of DOMART by 7.30 a.m. and CONDE FOLIE by 10.0 a.m.
Two field Ambulances from LONGUEVIL-LETTE.	Will follow ~~Sialkot~~ Lucknow Brigade.
Auxiliary Horse Transport Train.	Headquarters will accompany Divisional Headquarters.
Sanitary Section. Mobile Ambulance Workshop.	Via ST LEGER – FLIXECOURT – HANGEST and to be clear of DOMART by 9.0 a.m.
Dismounted men	Will march by Brigades and move after mounted troops are clear and will billet night 22nd/23rd in MOUFFLERS under Major Cook, 38th C.I. Horse, and move into their own Brigade areas on 23rd via HANGEST. On 23rd inst. CONDE FOLIE Bridge may not be used by 1st Indian Cavalry Division.
Divisional Report Centre.	Will close at DOMART at 10.0 a.m. and open at the same time at QUESNOY Chateau.

C.A.C. Godwin
Lieutenant Colonel,
General Staff, 1st Ind: Cav: Divn.

To

....

SECRET.   No. Q-5743.
Headquarters.
1st Indian Cavalry Division.
20th October 1915.

Administrative Instructions in connection with G.A.404.
----

1. Billeting areas are as follows :-

   Divisional Headquarters........LEQUESNOY. SOUES.

Divisional Troops.. ....

   One Field Ambulance............PICQUIGNY.
   Two   "   ....ST. MAULVIS. ANDAINVILLE.
   Divnl Ammunition Col...........LE MAZIS. LE QUESNE. ARGUEL.
   Divnl Ammunition Park..........   .EPAUMESNIL.
   Field Squadron.................LIOMER.
   Auxiliary H.T.Co...............TAILLY. LALEU.

Lucknow
~~Sialkot~~ Brigade................PICQUIGNY-FOUDRINOY-MOLLIENS VIDAMES-
                                   HALLIVILLERS-AUMONT (exclusive) -
Sialkot   LE FAYEL (exclusive) -SOUES (exclusive
                                   - CROUY (exclusive).

~~Lucknow~~ Brigade................CROUY-SOUES (exclusive) - LE FAYEL -
                                   BELLOY - ST LEONARDS - ETREJUST (exclu
                                   ive)- VERGIES - ALLERY (exclusive)-
                                   ARAINES (exclusive) HANGEST SUR SOMME.
                                   (LE QUESNOY excluded.)

Mhow Brigade...................... AUMONT-HORNOY- GUIBERMESNIL(exclusive)
                                   LIOMER (exclusive)-FRESNEVILLE-ETREJUS
Lucknow   BELLOY- ST LEONARD (exclusive)) -
                                   MERICOURT EN VIMEUX.

2. ~~Sialkot~~ Brigade will billet one Field Ambulance in PICQUIGNY, and reserve for them the house selected for a Hospital.

3. Details regarding villages are sent to the Brigades and Units affected

4. The rendezvous given in I.C.C. Q-1455 for 22nd and 23rd will be also the final R.V. at the hour stated.

5. All dismounted followers will accompany the D.M.   Orders regarding the moves of these parties will issue later.

6. All B echelon wagons have now been freed from iron rations, and are with units ready for use.

7. Horse rug wagons will be issued to units by O.C. A.S.C. on 21st as follows :-
              3 per regiment.
              1 per Battery
              1 for Field Squadron.
              1 for Divisional Headquarters.

                                        [signature]
                                        Lieutenant Colonel,
                                        A. A., and Q. M. G.,
                                        1st Indian Cavalry Division.

Secret

B.M. 84.   20th October 1915.

To the O.C. U Battery R.H.A.
        K.D.Gds
        29th Lrs
        36th J.H.
        Sig Troop
        Mob Vety Section.
    Bde Transport Officer.

Copy to 1st Indian Cavalry Division.

1. The Brigade will move to new billeting area on 22nd October.
Starting Point Six cross roads FIENVILLERS, at 8-30 a.m.

Order of march - Advanced Guard 1 Sqdn K.D.Gds.

    Main Body - Signal Troop
                K.D.Gds (less 1 sqdn).
                36th J.Horse.
    (29th Lrs) U Battery R.H.A.   ) under Major
                A echelon, in order of units) Lascelles
                                                      R.H.A.

2. B echelon and Mobile Veterinary Section will march under an officer to be detailed by O.C., K.D.Gds, and pass the same starting point in order of units at 7-30 a.m. This Column will halt in MONTRELET to allow the Brigade, U Battery and A echelon to pass

3. K.D.Gds and 36th J.Horse will water at CANAPLES, 29th Lancers at FIEFFES, U Battery and A echelon at MONTRELET.

4. On arrival of the Brigade at PICQUIGNY, units will march independently to their billeting areas.

5. Brigade Report Centre will close at MON PLAISIR at 10-0 a.m. and open at CAVILLON Chateau at the same hour.

                                                          A.M. Turner Major.
                                       Brigade Major, Lucknow Cavalry Brigade.

SECRET

B.M.86.   21st October 1915.

To the O.C. U Battery R.H.A.
         King's Dragoon Guards.
         29th Lancers.
         36th Jacob's Horse.
         Signal Troop.
         Mobile Veterinary Section.
    Brigade Transport Officer.

   Copy to 1st Indian Cavalry Division.

1. In supersession of my B.M.84 dated 20th inst., the Starting Point for fighting troops and A and B echelon of K.D.Gs and 36th J.H. will be BERNEUIL-FIENVILLERS and BERNAVILLE - CANAPLES cross roads. That of U Battery and 29th Lrs remains FIENVILLERS. The times of starting hold good.

2. The B echelon column will now water in CANAPLES, and be clear of that place by 9-30 a.m. The B echelon of 29th Lrs, U Battery, Bde H.Qrs and Mobile Vety Section will march to CANAPLES under an officer to be detailed by O.C 29th Lancers, who will report to Capt WELLS, K.D.Gds at CANAPLES Chateau.

3. Units will march independently from rendezvous as in para 1 to Brigade rendezvous at O in HALLOY les Pernois at 10-30 a.m. On their way to Brigade rendezvous units will water as follows:-

    K.D.Gds............ CANAPLES.
    36th J.H............HALLOY.
    29th Lrs............FIEFFES.

4. The A echelon of units will march with their units to water and afterwards to the Brigade Starting Point where they follow in rear of the Battery under the command of Major Lascelles R.H.A.

                                             Major.
              Brigade Major, Lucknow Cavalry Brigade.

SERIAL NO. 111.

Confidential

War Diary

of

Headquarters Lucknow Imperial Service Infantry Brigade

FROM 1st November 1915 TO (0) 30th November 1915.

Army Form C. 2118.

WAR DIARY
or
INTELLIGENCE SUMMARY.
(Erase heading not required.)

Instructions regarding War Diaries and Intelligence Summaries are contained in F.S. Regs., Part II, and the Staff Manual respectively. Title pages will be prepared in manuscript.

Hour, Date, Place.	Summary of Events and Information.	Remarks and references to Appendices.
CAVILLON Nov. 7th	The 1st Indian Cavalry Division paraded near Le QUESNOY for distribution of French decorations by the Corps Commander. The following officers, N.C.O.'s men of the Lucknow Brigade received decorations:- Maj. R.H. LASCELLES "U" Battery 5th Class Legion of Honour Capt. NOAKES " " Croix de Guerre Lieut A.W. DAVIS K.D.G. " Corpl. W. WATERMAN " " Dafadar SAYED HASSAN 38th J.H. " " Dafadar NURALI 29th L. "	CR 627 KJK 6 1/11/16
" 13th	The Indian Cavalry Corps paraded near Le QUESNOY for inspection by the III Army Commander.	
" 18th	The Corps billeting area having been reduced by III Army, the Brigade moved into closer billets w/ of line HANGEST- MONTAGNE. & went into billets as follows:- Brig H.Q. VIEULAINE, "U" Battery BETTENCOURT-RNG, LONGPRÉ 29th L. CONDÉ FOLIE - 38th FONTAINE, WANEL, SOREL, Met Rut CATELET. All horses were under cover but tightly packed. Permanent workforce made tight shelters for sufficient numbers as to give each horse lying down room no change.	
VIEULAINE " 31st		

Ou Gaan Maj. Brig Major.

No. Q-215

Headquarters.

1st Indian Cavalry Division.

17th November 1915.

MEMORANDUM.

1. The changes in the Billeting Area of the Division will take place tomorrow.

2. SIALKOT BRIGADE. 17th Lancers from HANGEST will move via AIRAINES - METIGNY to their new billets, and be clear of METIGNY by 11. a.m.
MONTAGNE to be clear of troops and transport by 10.a.m.

3. MHOW BRIGADE. MERICOURT to be clear of troops and transport by 10.a.m.

4. Field Ambulances to be clear of ST MAULVIS and ANDAINVILLE by 12. Noon.

5. Auxiliary Horse Transport Co. will march via any road East of AIRAINES - LONGPRE railway to their new billets, and be West of the CALAIS - PARIS road by 12. Noon.

6. LUCKNOW BRIGADE. May use any roads between the CALAIS-PARIS road (inclusive) and the road along the South of the SOMME (inclusive)
They will not be West of the line LONGPRE - MOLLIENS-CAMPS VIDAME before 12. Noon, and must be clear of the line HANGEST - MERICOURT by 4.p.m.

7. The Divisional Ammunition Park will be in AIRAINES and have all roads clear for the passage of troops by 9.30.a.m.

8. Formed bodies of troops may march through AIRAINES but no men with horses are to be allowed to stop in the town.

9. The Auxiliary Horse Transport Co. is detailing 14 G.S. Wagons for Lucknow Brigade and 6 for Sialkot Brigade to help in the move.

10. O.O.C. Lucknow will reserve space in his area for one Cav. Field Ambulance

W.C. Bruce Lieutenant Colonel,
A. A., and Q. M. G.,
1st Indian Cavalry Division.

To.
Brigades
O.C., A.S.C.
A.D.M.S.
O.C. 1st Ind R.H.A.Bde.

B.M. 242.

Copies to Regts & Btty.

No. B.M. 250   17th November 1916.

To the O.C., U Battery R.H.A.
             King's Dragoon Guards.
             29th Lancers.
             36th Jacob's Horse.
             Signal Troop.
             Mobile Vety Section.
        Bde Supply Officer
        "   Transport Officer.

    Copy to 1st Indian Cavalry Division.

1. Reference attached - Units will march independently to their new areas.

Routes. 2. 36th Horse via Le MESGE-CABARET (Le QUESNOY) - AIRAINES.
                To be West of the Cross roads CABARET by 1-0 p.m.

    Bde H.Qrs & Signal Troop via SOUES - CABARET (Le QUESNOY) -
            LONGPRE, to follow 36th Horse and be North of
            SOUES - AIRAINES road by 1-30 p.m.

    K.D.Gds via MONTAGNE and LE QUESNOY.
            They will not cross the SOUES - AIRAINES road
            before 1-0 p.m., but must be North of that road
            by 2-30 p.m.

    U Battery R.H.A. via SOUES - CABARET (Le QUESNOY), not to
            be West of SOUES before 2-30 p.m.

    29th Lancers via CROUY and HANGEST.

    Mobile Veterinary Section will follow 29th Lancers.

3. Brigade Report Centre will close at CAVILLON at 12 noon
and open at CHATEAU VIEULAINE at the same hour.

Office Copy

                                A.M.Turner
                                        Major.
                    Brigade Major, Lucknow Cavalry Brigade.

SERIAL NO. 111.

Confidential

War Diary

of

Headquarters, Lucknow Cavalry Brigade.

FROM 1st December 1915 TO 31st January 1916

Army Form C. 2118.

WAR DIARY
or
INTELLIGENCE SUMMARY.   LUCKNOW CAV. BDE

(Erase heading not required.)

Instructions regarding War Diaries and Intelligence Summaries are contained in F. S. Regs., Part II, and the Staff Manual respectively. Title pages will be prepared in manuscript.

Hour, Date, Place.	Summary of Events and Information.	Remarks and references to Appendices.
PICQUIGNY Dec 16th	The Brigade marched at 10.30am to new billeting area & went into billets as follows:- Brig H.Q. FRANLEU. K.D.G. QUESNOY — LE MONTANT — CAHON — 29th *SAIGNEVILLE — GOUY — CAHON. 38th *FRANLEU — CAMPAGNE — FRIREVILLES — HYPONVILLE M.V.S. FRIREVILLES. U Battery has left the Brigade and is now to be temporary attached to 51st Divn.	* Regt. H.Q. JRi[?] 26/3/16
Dec 14th	No change	
FRANLEU Dec 31st		

A.H.Fenwick[?] Maj
Brigade Major Lucknow Brigade

Army Form C. 2118.

WAR DIARY
or
INTELLIGENCE SUMMARY.
(Erase heading not required.)

Instructions regarding War Diaries and Intelligence Summaries are contained in F.S. Regs., Part II, and the Staff Manual respectively. Title pages will be prepared in manuscript.

Hour, Date, Place.	Summary of Events and Information.	Remarks and references to Appendices.
FRANLEU Jan 5th 1916.		
10th	Lt. R.D OWEN JONES accidentally killed in a bombing accident. Outline scheme issued by D.W. for assembly of the 3 Regt. Machine Gun detachments under a Commander, as a Machine Gun Squadron.	
28th	Capt. M.M. CARPENDALE temporarily appointed to command Lucknow Bde. Machine Gun Squadron. Machine Gun Dets assembled in billets in QUESNOY.	
31st	LE-MONTANT - horses in the RAPERIE.	
31st	An Indian digging party consisting of 2/Lt R.H. RICE 5S. O.R. 29th Lancers & 2/Lt A.W. HARRISON & 55. O.R. 36th Jacob's Horse entrained at GAMACHES & proceeded to join the 37th Div. They were billeted in LAHERDERE.	

A.M. Anmenstrey
Brigadier, Lucknow Bde.

<u>SECRET.</u> HQ

No. Q-3275

Indian Cavalry Corps

13th December 1915

Reference Operation Order No.11 dated 13th December 1915 -

1. LUCKNOW Casualty Clearing Station will move to FRESSENNEVILLE by 6 p.m. on 14th December. D.D.M.S. will report completion - Till the 17th inclusive their traffic to and from LONGPRE will be via CAMBRON - PONT REMY - LIERCOURT.

2. The Corps Troops Supply Column will deliver 2 days supplies by the evening of 15th at the new billets of the JODHPUR Lancers, No 3 Battery Armoured Cars, and detachment of Corps Signal Squadron; lorries will then return to HALLENCOURT.

3. The billetting of No 3 Battery Armoured Cars will be controlled by the Senior Special Service Officer with JODHPUR LANCERS.

4. No 25 Ordnance Workshop will move at 1.30 p.m. on 17th via OISEMONT and LE TRANSLAY.

5. MEERUT Reserve Park and the Field Remount Section will assemble at AIRAINES and march at 8 a.m. on 18th December via OISEMONT and LE TRANSLAY.

6. The 1st Indian Cavalry Ammunition Park and Advanced Depot Medical Stores will be billetted under orders of O.C. MEERUT Reserve Park and will occupy the North portion of BOUILLANCOURT; its lorries will move in and out only through BUSMENARD and HINFRAY.

7. MONTIERES will not be occupied at present.

8. The Sections of the Indian Cavalry Supply Columns which load at LONGPRE on 17th December will move after loading to their new billets, the 1st Indian Cavalry Supply Column leaving AIRAINES at 2 p.m. followed by the 2nd Indian Cavalry Supply Column half an hour later. Lorries of the Indian Cavalry Corps Troops Supply Column after loading at LONPRE on 17th morning will move direct to GAMACHES via OISEMONT.

9.

9. On 17th December Sections of Supply Columns which are delivering to troops will move to Brigade rendezvous as appointed by each Division.

   The 1st Indian Cavalry Supply Column will move via Route Nationale No 1 and BRAY - les - MAREUIL, leaving AIRAINES at 9.30 a.m: the 2nd Indian Cavalry Supply Column will leave AIRAINES by convenient routes at 12 noon. On completion of issues Sections will proceed to their new billets.

   Vehicles of the Indian Cavalry Corps Troops Supply Column will leave HALLENCOURT at 1.30 p.m.

10. On the 16th and 17th December Ordnance lorries will accompany Supply Columns and the movements of postal lorries will be adjusted by A.D. Postal Services to suit the convenience of troops.

    Ammunition Parks will be moved by Divisional arrangements.

11. The usual action will be taken by all units to endeavour to adjust claims before leaving billets.

12. Divisions will report to Corps Headquarters as soon as ever they have fixed billets for Supply Columns, to permit of early issue of any necessary orders controlling motor traffic in and out of BLANGY. Route Nationale No 15 between GAMACHES and BOUTTENCOURT will not be used by lorries, nor for exercising horses in draught.

13. Advanced Depot Medical Stores will be moved by train to new Railhead.

14. No billets will be occupied in BLANGY by any details of the Indian Cavalry Corps.

J. Russell-Kerr
Brigadier-General,
D.A. & Q.M.G. Indian Cavalry Corps.

S E C R E T. Headquarters 1st Indian Cavalry Division,

14th December 1915.

No.Q-593. ADMINISTRATIVE INSTRUCTIONS.

Reference Indian Cavalry Corps Administrative Orders, No.Q-3215, dated 13th December 1915.

Billeting Areas are as follows :-

Divl. Headquarters.	.. DARGNIES.
1st Indian R.H.A.Bde.)	.. BEAUCHAMPS.
Divl. Ammn. Column.)	
Divl. Ammn. Park.	.. BOUILLANCOURT (billeted by Corps H.Q)
Field Squadron.	.. EMBRLVILLE.
Supply Column.	.. BOUVAINCOURT.
Sialkot Field Ambulance.	.. TOEUFLES. (billeted by Sialkot Bde).
Lucknow Field Ambulance.)	
Ambala Field Ambulance.)	
Sanitary Section.)	BUIGNY.
Motor Ambulance Workshop.)	
Auxiliary Horse Transport Coy.-	VALINES or CHEPY. (To be billeted by Mhow Bde).

Sialkot Bde.   .. LAMBERCOURT - BIENFAY - Route 28 to BAINAST - TRINQUIS exclusive - ACHEUX - FRIERES.

Lucknow Bde.   .. SAIGNEVILLE - CAHON - MIANNAY (exclusive) - HAVRE - LILLE Route to St.MARC (exclusive) - FRANLEU.

Mhow Bde.   .. SAUCOURT - MONCHAUX - CHEPY - FEUQUIERES - FRESSENNEVILLE.

2. D.M. of the Lucknow Brigade will move by train from LONGPRE on 16th : time and station of destination will be notified later.

3. D.M. of Sialkot and Mhow Brigades will be conveyed to the new area in lorries on 15th. 5 lorries per unit will rendezvous at a regimental H.Q. at 9.0.a.m. on that date.

4. D.M. will take with them their kit, rations for consumption on the 15th and 16th, and also the extra day's ration which is in regimental charge for these men.

5. In order to set free lorries for this purpose, rations for all units for consumption on the 16th will be delivered about noon on the 14th to the extent to which units can carry them. Units should take as much of the ration for the 15th as they can, that is, all the mens' ration, all the grain except the evening feed, and enough hay to last them till the hour of marching.

6. G.O.C.Mhow Bde. will billet the Auxiliary Horse Transport Coy. either at the South East end of VALINES or the North West end of CHEPY, as their work will be chiefly at the railway station between those villages.

7. The Lucknow Casualty Clearing Station is billeted in FRESSENNEVILLE in two empty chateaux on the North side of the

main

main HAVRE - LILLE road. The remainder of that street to the East of the Chateaux and Usine opposite has been allotted for billeting accommodation.

8. G.O.C. Sialkot Bde. will reserve for the Sialkot Fd. Ambulance an old farm Chateau on the Western side of TOEUFLES, which will be used as a hospital, and also sufficient billets for that Field Ambulance, i.e., 5 Officers, 60 British, 110 Indian and 70 horses.

9. Sialkot Field Ambulance will move on 15th: and Ambala Field Ambulance on 17th. Times of movement will be notified later.

10. The road leading from DARGNIES to FEUQUIERES is impassable for motor traffic.

W K Browne
Lieut-Colonel,
A.A. & Q.M.G., 1st Indian Cavalry Division.

No G - 293.

Headquarters,
1st Indian Cavalry Division.
14th December 1915.

MEMORANDUM.

The Division will move to its new billeting area, as allotted in Administrative instructions, No. Q-593, dated 14th December as follows :-

Lucknow Brigade.	By any roads North of the AIRAINES, cross roads ½ mile South West of DUNCQ, BRAY-les-MAREUIL, MAREUIL, CAMBRON MIANNAY road, inclusive.
Mhow Brigade.	By any roads South of the FRESNEVILLE, OISEMONT, ST MAXENT, TOURS Road inclusive.
Sialkot Brigade and "Q" R.H.A.	By any roads between the Southern road allotted to Lucknow Brigade and the Northern road allotted to Mhow Brigade, both exclusive. 17th Lancers to be North of the FRESNEVILLE OISEMONT Road by 9.0 a.m.
Field Squadron & Divl. Ammn. Column	Under the orders of the Officer Commanding Field Squadron, R.E. by SENAPPONT, BOUTTENCOURT, GAMACHES Road.
Divl. Headqtrs.	By AIRAINES, OISEMONT, GAMACHES, BEAUCHAMPS Road to DARGNIES, leaving LE QUESNOY at 8.0 a.m.
Headqtrs, Aux: Horse Transport Coy.	Will follow Divisional Headquarters to OISEMONT, thence by ST MAXENT, FEUQUIERES to billets allotted by Mhow Brigade.
Headqtrs, 1st Ind. R.H.A. Bde.	By OISEMONT and GAMACHES.
Lucknow Cavalry Field Ambulance.	By HALLENCOURT, ST MAXIENT, MAISNIERES Road To give way to any troops either passing or crossing it.
Ambala Cavalry Field Ambulance.	On 17th December, as per Administrative Instructions.
Sialkot Cavalry Field Ambulance.	On 15th December, as per Administrative Instructions.
Divisional Ammunition Park.	By OISEMONT, GAMACHES, BEAUCHAMPS Road Not to leave AIRAINES before 12 noon.
Divisional Supply Column.	As per Administrative Instructions.
Dismounted men.	As per Administrative Instructions.

2. Report Centre will close at LE QUESNOY at 11.0 a.m. and open at DARGNIES at the same hour.

H.E. Macfarlane
Captain,
General Staff, 1st I. C. D.

No. B.M. 485   Headquarters, Lucknow Cavalry Bde.
                                15th December 1915.

To the O.C. King's Dragoon Guards,
          29th Lancers.
          36th Jacob's Horse.
          Signal Troop.
          Mobile Veterinary Section.
     Brigade Supply Officer.
     Brigade Transport Officer.

1.   Reference the attached, the Brigade will march at 10-30 a.m. tomorrow via LIERCOURT, BRAY, MAREUIL to CAMBRON, whence units will proceed independently to their areas.
     Starting Point - Cross roads ½ mile S.W. of DUNCQ at 10-30 a.m.
     Order of March - Advd Guard   1 Sqdn 36th J.Horse
                      Main Body   Signal Troop
                                   36th J.Horse (less 1 sqdn)
                                   K.D.Gds.
                                   29th Lancers
                                   A echelon in order of units
                                   Mob.Vety Section.

2.   The Brigade will halt to water at CAUBERT-MAREUIL.

3.   B echelon will march at 9-30 a.m. under the Brigade Transport Officer, in order of units.
     Starting Point - Cross roads ½ Mile S.W. of DUNCQ.

4.   B echelon will halt to water and feed at BRAY, where the Brigade will pass it. Care should be taken to keep the road clear.

5.   Report Centre will close at VIEULAINE at 11-0 a.m., and open at the Chateau at S.E. exit of FRANLEU at the same hour.

                                              Major.
                              Brigade Major, Lucknow Cavalry Brigade.

Copy to :-
      1st Indian Cavalry Division.

SERIAL NO. 111

Confidential

Cavalry Diary

of

Headquarters, Lucknow Cavalry Brigade

FROM 1st February 1916 TO 30th April 1916

Army Form C. 2118.

WAR DIARY
or
INTELLIGENCE SUMMARY. Lucknow Cav.

(Erase heading not required.)

Instructions regarding War Diaries and Intelligence Summaries are contained in F. S. Regs., Part II, and the Staff Manual respectively. Title pages will be prepared in manuscript.

Hour, Date, Place.	Summary of Events and Information.	Remarks and references to Appendices.
FRANCE. Feb. 3rd 7th	"U" Battery rejoined the Brigade from billets in OCHAINCOURT.	
" 17th	Two dipping parties from K.D.G.'s entrained at GAMACHES Lt MUIR + 35 O.R. to proceed to 48th Div. 75 Cops. Lt. CARD " " 36th Div. 175 Cops.	
" 28th	The Lucknow dipping party which left the Brigade on 31.1.16 for attachment to 37th Div. rejoined the Brigade	
" 29th	No change	

Antomer Hay
B.M. Lucknow Cav. Bde.

Army Form O. 2118.

WAR DIARY

or

INTELLIGENCE SUMMARY. Lucknow Cav. Brigade

(Erase heading not required.)

Instructions regarding War Diaries and Intelligence Summaries are contained in F. S. Regs., Part II, and the Staff Manual respectively. Title pages will be prepared in manuscript.

Hour, Date, Place.	Summary of Events and Information.	Remarks and references to Appendices.
March 8th FRANLEU	Capt. Z.G. BURMESTER 38 Lancers joined Brigade Staff for instruction.	
10th "	The Baston Digging Party under Lt Cadir K.D.G rejoined Brigade from 38th Lans	
20th "	The digging party under Lt. Mills K.D.G rejoined from 46th Divn	
28th "	The Brigade marched to a new billeting area under orders attached & here into billets as follows:- B. H.Q VAUX — U" Battery TOULENT- K.D.G GUSSCHAUT. 29 F Lancers FONTAINE L'ETALON & CHEPIENNE - 38 facts Lancers BOUFFLERS & GENNE - IVERGNY Machine Gun Sqdn CAUMONT Mot. M.G. LUMBRVILLE. Remained in the New area the following Lancers being attached to the Brigade vizt Field in LEPLANCHIEL	
30th VAUX	No Change	

AnLumsden
B.M.

B.M. 497.   25-3-16.

To K.D.Gds.
   29th Lrs.
   Jodhpur Lrs.
   M.G.Sqdn.

   Reference para 3 March Orders dated 24-3-16.

   Dismounted men, numbers as follows will rendez-vous at CAMBRON, E exit, at 9-30 a.m. on 26th inst.
   They will be marched by the senior British officer to the Main Station at ABBEVILLE, and must arrive there before 11-0 a.m.
   Lieut. CARD, K.D.Gds will report to R.T.O. Main Station, ABBEVILLE, at 10-0 a.m. 26th instant, and hand in statement of strengths as given hereon.
   No kit beyond equipment will be taken.
   On arrival at AUXI le CHATEAU at 13-10 hours, parties will be marched direct to billeting areas.

K.D.Gds and M.G.S.   Offrs 1   O.R. 103.
29th Lancers   "   1   "   25
Jodhpur Lrs   "   1   "   89
                                      108

   Numbers given above must be adhered to by units.

                                            Captain.
   for Brigade Major, Lucknow Cavalry Brigade.

"A" Form. Army Form C. 2121.
MESSAGES AND SIGNALS.
No. of Message..........

Prefix .... Code .... m.	Words	Charge	This message is on a/c of:	Recd. at................m
Office of Origin and Service Instructions.	Sent		.... Service.	Date..................
....	At...........m.			From..................
....	To			
....	By		(Signature of "Franking Officer.")	By..................

TO {				

*	Sender's Number.	Day of Month.	In reply to Number.	A A A

From	
Place	
Time	

The above may be forwarded as now corrected.   **(Z)**

....
Censor.   Signature of Addressor or person authorised to telegraph in his name.

* This line should be erased if not required.

225,000. W 14042—M 44. H. W. & V., Ld. 12/15.

Copy No. 15

March Orders by Brig-General W.H.FASKEN, C.B.,
Commanding Lucknow Cavalry Brigade.

24-3-16.

Reference 1/100,000 Map, Sheets 11 and 14.

1. The Brigade will march on 26-3-16 to new area via BUIGNY, LE PLESSIEL and CANCHY, in 3 columns
   The commanders of (b) and (c) columns will make their own staff arrangements.
   (a) Mounted troops.
       Rendezvous (Advanced Guard 1 sqdn 29th Lrs, ABBEY, 10-0 a.m.
                 (Main body, S exit BONNEVAL, 10-0 a.m.
       Order of march - Signal Troop
                     29th Lrs.(less 1 sqdn.)
                     M.G.Sqdn.
                     36th.J.Horse
                     Jodhpur Lrs.
                     K.D.Gds.

   29th Lrs, M.G.Sqdn, and K.D.Gds. will march to rendezvous via GOUY, Pt PORT, level crossing at de of BOIS de BONNANCE.
       K.D.Gds. must halt with head just W of GD.LAVIERS till 36th J.H. and Jodhpur Lrs. are clear of that point.
       36th J.H. followed by Jodhpur Lrs. will march to starting point via CAMBRON.
   (b) Wheeled column (under Major Lascelles R.H.A.) starting point GD.LAVIERS, 10-30 a.m.
       A Echelons of 29th.Lrs, M.G.S., and K.D.Gds. will follow K.D.Gds. as far as S in LES AMOURETTES where they will water and then close up with head at the church at GD.LAVIERS on the PORT le GRAND-GD. LAVIERS road.
       U Battery followed by A Echelons of 36th J.H., B.H.Qrs, Jodhpur Lrs, also by Jodhpur Lrs Field Ambulance and M.V.Section will rendezvous in that order at the level crossing just S. of GD.LAVIERS at 10-0 a.m. Horses will be watered.
       As soon as the watering is complete the wheeled column will move off in the following order - U Btty R.H.A., A Echelons of 29th Lrs, M.G.Sqdn, 36th J.H., B.H.Qrs., Jodhpur Lrs, and Jodhpur Lrs. Field Ambulance, M.V.Section, K.D.Gds, and march via THUISON, Pt 67, CANCHY and disperse in the same order as that laid down for units in paragraph 2.
       Cyclists will march as a formed body in rear of A Echelon.
   (c) B Echelon (under Lieut. E.S.Kingsell, B.T.O.) starting point fork roads just S.E. of N in CAMBRON, 8-0 a.m.
       29th Lrs, M.G.Sqdn and K.D.Gds. on the GOUY-CAMBRON road, U Btty 36th J.H., B.H.Qrs, Jodhpur Lrs. on the MIANNAY-CAMBRON road.
       The column will move off in the following order - 29th Lrs, M.G.S., U Btty R.H.A., 36th J.H., B.H.Qrs., Jodhpur Lrs, K.D.Gds, and march by the route laid down for A Echelon. Column will water in CANCHY, turning off main road into the village to do so, and halting until the mounted column and A Echelon have passed.

2. DISPERSAL On arrival at cross roads N.E. of E in FONTAINE sur MAYE, 29th Lrs, M.G.S., 36th J.H., will move to billets via Le BOISLE, remaining units via GUESCHART.
       Transport will disperse in the same way.

3. DISMOUNTED MEN (less those left with dumped stores) will entrain at ABBEVILLE at 11-0 a.m. on the 26th instant under separate orders.

P. T. O.

4. **MARCH DISCIPLINE.** On arriving at any level crossing each unit will detail an officer and an interpreter to control traffic. If barriers are closed, sections will be formed and the line crossed in that formation as soon as the barrier opens. Lost distance must be regained by moving up in formed bodies and not by individuals increasing their pace as they think fit.

5. **SALVAGE TROOP.** O.C. Salvage Troop will visit all billeting areas on 26th instant, collect salvage parties at GOUY at 8-0 a.m. on 27th instant, and march to new area.

6. **REPORT CENTRE** closes FRANLEU 8-0 a.m. 26th, and opens VAULX same hour.

Issued at 3-15 p.m.

E.B. Beresford Captain.
for Brigade Major, Lucknow Cavalry Bde.

Copy No.   to U.R.H.A.
               K.D.Gds
               29th L.
               36th J.H.
               Jodh.Lrs
               M.G.S.
               M.V.S.
               Sig.Troop
               B.S.O.
               B.T.O.
               B.V.O.
               B.Sal.Troop
               1st I.C.Div.
               Bde Staff
               Filed.

Secret

Copy No...... 4.

1st Indian Cavalry Division Operation Order No. 20.

Dated 21st March 1916.

Reference Maps 1/100,000. Sheets ABBEVILLE and LENS.
1/ 80,000   "   "   A

1. The Division will move to the new area as in attached March Table.

2. Movements to commence on 24th instant, and to be completed by 26th instant.

3. Divisional Troops (less Sanitary Section, SIALKOT Cavalry Field Ambulance and Divisional Ammunition Park), under command of O.C. Field Squadron, will pass the starting point in the following order on 25th instant:-

Divl. Headquarters. Signal Squadron. Field Squadron.	8.30. a.m.	Starting point - Divl. HdQrs. CHATEAU, DARGNIES.
1st Ind. R.H.A. Bde. HdQrs. Divl. Ammunition Column.	....	To join via FRANLEU.
Field Ambulances (less SIALKOT C.F.A) Motor Amblce. Workshop.	8.45. a.m.	

4. A Divl. Staff Officer will allot billets for Divl. Troops on 25/26th.

5. Arrival reports on 24th and 25th to be submitted.

6. Report Centre closes at DARGNIES at 12 noon, 25th, and opens at same hour at Chau at WAIL.

C.A.C. Godwin
Lieut-Colonel,
General Staff,
1st Indian Cavalry Division.

Issued at 2.0. p.m.

    Copy. No. 1...   Third Army.
    "   "   2 ...   Sialkot Bde.
    "   "   3.   Mhow Bde.
    "   "   4.   Lucknow Bde.
    "   "   5.   1st Ind. R.H.A. Bde.
    "   "   6.   Field Squadron.
    "   "   7.   Signal Squadron.
    "   "   8.   O.C.A.S.C.
    "   "   9.   S.S.O.
    "   " 10.   A.D.M.S.
    "   " 11.   A.D.V.S.
    "   " 12.   D.A.D.O.S.
    "   " 13.   Camp Comdt.
    "   " 14.   Liaison Officer.
    "   " 15.   Jodhpur Lancers.
    "   " 16.& 17. "Q".
    "   " 18-21.   File. Diary & Office.
    "   " 22   2nd Ind. Cav. Div

MARCH TABLE.

Unit.	24th March. Route & Destination.		25th March. Route & Destination.	26th March.
SIALKOT Bde with SIALKOT C.F.A. attached	CAMBRON,ABBEVILLE,ST.RI-QUIER to billeting area NEUILLY-LE-DIEN, Mson. PONTHIEU,HIERMONT,BERNATRE.	To be clear of ABBEVILLE by 11.0.a.m.	To new billeting area.	
MHOW Bde.	CAMBRON,ABBEVILLE,to billeting area ONEUX,ST.RI-QUIER,NEUFMOULIN.	Not to enter ABBEVILLE till 11.a.m.	To new billeting area.	
JODHPUR LANCERS.	TILLOY,TOURS-EN-VIMEUX, TOEUFLES to billets at MIANNAY.	Not to enter MIANNAY till 2.0.p.m. The PORT-ELETTE Railway Crossing will not be used.		
LUCKNOW Bde with JODHPUR LANCERS attd.			Any crossing West of ABBEVILLE exclusive, avoiding ABBEVILLE, via CANCHY,GUESCHART to new billeting area.	
DIVISIONAL TROOPS, (less Sanitary Section, SIALKOT Cav.Fd.Amblce. & Divl.Ammn.Park).			CAMBRON,ABBEVILLE to billeting area,ONEUX ST.RIQUIER, NEUFMOULIN.	To new billeting area.
DIVL.AMMUNITION PARK.				To new billeting area.

WAR DIARY
or
INTELLIGENCE SUMMARY.

(Erase heading not required.)

Army Form C. 2118.

Lucknow Bgde / Lucknow Cavalry Brigade

Hour, Date, Place.	Summary of Events and Information.	Remarks and references to Appendices.
April 9th VAULX	The Brigade moved to a Training area N of ST RIQUIER & went into billets as follows:- BHQ YVRENCH, K.D.Gs NEUF MOULIN, 2g Lancers YVRENCH & YVRENCHEUX, & Battery & Jodhpur Lancers ARGENVILLERS. S&T fields. Horses & M.G. Sqdn GAPENUE	
" 15th YVRENCH	Brigade returned to permanent billeting area	
" 19 "	Capt A.H.A. EMPSON 28th Cavalry appointed Bgde Signalling Officer in succession to Capt MACKINTOSH appointed Staff Capt. Leavy clothing 17 F Caps.	
" 29th VAULX	One to Lt Col Huse from war troops issued to remts.	
" 30 "	No change	

Ancluenton
B.M. Luckuow Cav Bde.

SERIAL NO. 111

Confidential War Diary of

Headquarters, Lucknow Cavalry Brigade.

FROM 1st May 1916 TO 30th June 1916.

WAR DIARY 4th NOW CAV. BDE.

Army Form C. 2118.

or

INTELLIGENCE SUMMARY.

(Erase heading not required.)

Instructions regarding War Diaries and Intelligence Summaries are contained in F. S. Regs., Part II, and the Staff Manual respectively. Title page will be prepared in manuscript.

Hour, Date, Place.	Summary of Events and Information.	Remarks and references to Appendices
May 1st VAULX	Brigade marched to Training Area for Divisional Training. Troops billeted as follows: Bde. H.Q. K.D.Gs. 365th forty fourth Coy. M.V.S. ST RIQUIER — 29th ONEUX — M.G. Sqdn. LEFESTEL	
" 4th ST RIQUIER	The Division was inspected by G.O.C. Reserve Corps.	
" 7th "	The Brigade returned to billeting area about VAULX.	
" 10th VAULX	Brigade moved to new billeting area about PREVENT & was billeted as follows Bde Hq. & Battery, forty four Lancers REBREUVE — K.D.Gs SERICOURT (HQ) SIBIVILLE 29th L. CANETTEMONT — 365th MONCHEAUX — M.G. Sqdns. M.V.S. HONVAL	
"13th REBREUVE	Brig. Gen. M F GAGE, D.S.O. assumed command of the Brigade vice Col. W. H. FASKEN, C.B.	
" 16th	"U" Battery left for attachment to 57th Div. Front	
" 17th	into action N.E. of MONT ST ELOI. HQ. BERTHONVAL FM	
" 23rd	Bde paid a two day visit to inspect all units, mounted in turn	
31st	& commander in Chief inspected Artillery areas. No change	

An Fitzgerald Major Brigade

Army Form C. 2118.

WAR DIARY LUCKNOW BRIGADE
or
INTELLIGENCE SUMMARY.
(Erase heading not required.)

Instructions regarding War Diaries and Intelligence Summaries are contained in F. S. Regs., Part II, and the Staff Manual respectively. Title pages will be prepared in manuscript.

Hour, Date, Place.	Summary of Events and Information.	Remarks and references to Appendices
June 15th REBREUVE	50 men K.D.G's under 2/Lt J.P.BREWER proceeded by bus for attachment to 51st Div 17th Corps as Div.ng party.	
16th "	CAPT. R.S. SPURRIER, Lt H.S. HATFIELD, Lt R.G. FOX, 2/Lt S.L. PEACOCK & 200 men K.D.G's proceeded by lorry to SOUASTRE for work in XVII Corps area.	
18th "	MAJ. MAUNSELL & 300 men 36th J.H proceeded with No 1 working party by lorry to MONT ST ELOI for attachment to 51st Div.	
16th "	MAJ. BIRCH & 300 men 29th Lancers proceeded with No 2 working party by lorry to MAROEUIL for attachment to 51st Div.	
18th "	Capt J.S.D. GAGE 1st Hants Yeomanry joined as A.D.C. vice Lt. C.F.L. STEVENS, 10th Lancers	
26th "	4 Hotchkiss guns & detachments from 36th & 29th joined No 1 & 2 working parties, the horses were brought back to permanent billets.	
26th "	Capt SPURRIER & working party of 200 men K.D.G's rejoined Brigade	

WAR DIARY LUCKNOW. CAV. Bde.

or

INTELLIGENCE SUMMARY.

(Erase heading not required.)

Army Form C. 2118.

Hour, Date, Place.	Summary of Events and Information.	Remarks and references to Appendices
June 28th REBREUVE 30 F	The remaining working parties rejoined Brigade from XIII Corps. Brigade concentrated in close billets as follows :- B.H.Q. K.D.G. 7 M.Gs GROUCHES - 29th Lancers MILLY - 36 Jacob's Horse BOUT duo PRES M.G. Squadron LA FOSSE FM. Units marched independently via BOUQUEMAISON. Transport divided into A(1) Echelon (pack) - A(2) Echelon (wheel) "B" Echelon was organised under Scale 'A'(mobile) & Scale 'B' (special when ordered). See appendix attached. Jodhpur Lancers transferred from Lucknow Brigade to Divisional Troops.	

Ant Turner Major
Brigade Major.

SECRET.   No. G-899.   Headquarters 1st Indian Cavalry Division,
                                         28th June 1916.

To Bdes & Units of Divl Troops.
_____

1. The Division will move to the new area on the 30th instant as follows:-

   JODHPUR LANCERS –   via LE SOUICH to BREVILLERS – to be clear of
                       REBREUVIETTE by 9.0.a.m.

   MHOW Bde.-   via LUCHEUX, HALLOY to billets at AUTHIEULE –
                       to be clear of LUCHEUX by 10.0.a.m.

   SIALKOT Bde.-   via BEAUDRICOURT to billets at LUCHEUX – not
                       to enter LUCHEUX till 10.0.a.m. – to keep main
                       DOULLENS road clear after 11.0.a.m.

   DIVL. HEADQRS.)   Commander Major W. EVANS, R.E.
   SIGNAL SQUADRON.)
   FIELD SQUADRON.) Starting Point – Western exit of LE CAUROY at
                       9.30.a.m. – via BEAUDRICOURT, LUCHEUX to DOULLENS.
                       FIELD SQUADRON to billet at LE MARAIS SEC.

   LUCKNOW Bde.-   via BOUQUEMAISON to billets at GROUCHES,
                       BOUT DES PRES, MILLY and LA FOLIE Fm – not to
                       enter REBREUVIETTE till 9.30.a.m.

   1ST IND. R.H.A. BDE) Will march under orders of C.R.H.A. to
   DIVL. AMMN. COL.   ) DOULLENS – after 12 noon.

   FIELD AMBLCES.   ) via ARBRE, HTE VISEE to DOULLENS – not to
   less Motor Vehicles) enter REBREUVIETTE till 10.30.a.m.

   MOTOR VEHICLES of) to move to DOULLENS via XXXXXXX HTE VISEE
   Field Amblces.   ) at 3.0.p.m.

   DIVL. AMMN. PARK.- To move to DOULLENS via FREVENT at 4.0.p.m.

   AUX. HORSE TPT. COY.- To move to CCCOCHES at 1.0.p.m.

   DIVL SUPPLY COLUMN – remains at Gd. BOURET.

                                    and Field Sqdn.
2. Dismounted men of the 10 Regiments/to concentrate in REBREUVE
   at 3.0.p.m. – Major Sir T. TANCRED, Bart, will command the party.

3. Report Centre will close at LE CAUROY at 10.0.a.m. and open at
   DOULLENS at the same hour.

                                         W K Brown Lt Col
                                            for
                                         General Staff,
                                         1st Indian Cavalry Division.

SCALE 'A' MOBILE L.G.S.W.

FORE LIMBER

Nos.	Articles	lbs. Weight
1	Very Pistol	3
1	Box Flare Lights	29
1	Box Ammn. Very	14
1	Vety. Chest	25
2	Discs Sigs.	6
4	Mallets	10
2	Trench Stretchers	12
	Butchers Impl.	37
	Horse Gear and Drivers Kits	50
	Rifles (2)	17
3	Boxes Grenades	72
4	Lanterns Tent folding	30
6	Camp Kettles	48
1	Farrier's Tool Bag	14
	Horse Shoes and Nails (in sack)	100
	Pioneer Equipt.	
) 5	Gloves 5 pairs	
(1 n	Hammer	7
)	Cordage Tarred	10
(	Lashings 1½" 50'	
)	1" 20'	15
(	2" 48'	
) 1	Tape Measure	1
(	Rule, Set Square,	
)	Spanners 2, Files	5
(	2, Nails	
) 1	Auger	2
(5	Saws	10
) 1	Maul	10
(10	Hooks Bill	20
3	Boxes S.A.A.	225
1	Saddler's Repairing Kit	12
	Tarpaulin Pulley	40
	Ration Packs	48
	Grains for Team	64
		936

REAR LIMBER

Nos.	Articles	lbs. Weight
200	Bags Sand	128
10	Shovels	35
4	Picks	30
4	Picks Helves	8
1	Gal Rifle Oil	
	66 yds Flannellette)	
	50 Pull Through) Strings)	10
1	S.A.A. Boxes	75
	Rope 20 Fathoms	36
	Horse Shoes and Nails in sacks.	100
		422
	10 Axes Hand	20
		442

Ø Indian Regts equivalent weight cooking pots.

Note smaller articles of pioneer equipment are to be carried in some form of improvised wallet the leather bags being used as laid down in Q 2463 d 15.6.16, para 7.

SCALE 'B'
Add Oats 960 lbs.

Oats for Regtl. Hd. Qrs. to be carried on Hotchkiss limber

TABLE OF DISTRIBUTION OF TOOLS 'A' ECHELON.

3 TROOP MULES Load Table per mule.			Nos. per Sqdn pack	Nos per Regtl pack.	Totals for 4 L.@.S.W's	Totals for Regt.
Weight lbs.	Tools etc.	Nos. per mule.				
6	Axes Felling	1	3	12	0	12
30	Axes Pick	4	12	48	16	64
	Picks Helves	0	0	0	16	16
4	Axes Hand	2	6	24	40	64
35	Shovels G.S.	10	30	120	40	160
1	Hooks Reaping	1	3	12	0	12
4	Hooks Bill	2	6	24	40	64
48	Bags Ent.Tools	2	6	24	0	24
16	Bags Sand	25	75	300	800	1000
8	Kettles Camp	1	3	12	24	36
24	Grenades Box	1	3	12	12	24
2	Saws Hand	1	3	12	20	32
	Gloves Hedgers: pairs.	1	3	12	20	32
178						
62	Saddles Pack					
240						

Explosives Mules as per Divisional No. Q-2463 para 4.

Guncotton, wet, charges 15 oz.		96.
" dry primers.		240.
Detonators.		144.
Fuze, instantaneous.	yds.	300.
" safety	fathoms.	72.
Matches		468.
Bar boring or crow-bar.		1.
Hammers, about 7 lbs.		1.
Pliers.		2.
Twine.	lbs.	2.
Wire.	"	6.

MARCHING ORDER (Summer) SCALE 'A'.

Order put on.	Detail - On the Man.	lbs.	ozs.
1.	Haversack containing 2 gas helmets, 1 pair goggles	2	12
2.	Haversack containing Note book. Map. Rations, (unexpended portion).	2	12
3.	Waterbottle (full).	3	14
4.	Field Glasses	2	—
	Bayonet (attached to waist belt) both included.	2	3 ¾
	Field Dressing		2 ½
	Wire Cutters	1	3 ½
	Bandolier and 90 rounds S.A.A.	7	3
	Total Weight on man	22	2 ¾

Detail on Horse.

	Detail	lbs.	ozs.
	In Wallets.		
	1 Mug		6
	1 Handkerchief		2
	1 Pair Socks		4 ¼
	1 Towel		9
	1 Housewife		3 ½
	1 Holdhall, containing 1 piece soap, tooth brush, comb, shaving brush, razor in case, laces, knife, fork, spoon.	1	6 ½
	Iron Ration	2	6 ½
	2 oz. tin of Grease		2
	Over Wallets.		
	Waterproof Sheet	2	8
	Hay Net		7
	Mallet (1 per section) ?		
	Behind Saddle.		
	Coat W.B.	8	
	On Sword.		
	1 peg (picketing)	1	4
	Body Brush		10
	1 Surcingle Pad		10
∅/	**On Near Side.**		
	Nosebag (4lbs oats)	5	
	Shoe Case with 2 shoes and nails.	1	8
	Sword with Scabbard	4	8
∅/	**On Off Side.**		
	Rifle	8	15 ¾
	Mess Tin	1	6
	Water Bucket (on rifle bucket)	1	4
	Second Nosebag (4 lbs oats)	5	
	Round Horses Neck.		
	Bandolier, with 90 rounds S.A.A.	7	3
	Built-up 4ope	1	1
	Head Rope	1	1
	Saddlery etc.		
	"U.P" Saddle, panels, girth, stirrup irons, leathers, surcingle, wallets, rifle bucket.	31	
	Headcollar, Bit, Bridle, etc.		
	1 Blanket		
	Lance	4	
	Total Weight on Horse	90	13 ½
	Total Weight on Man	22	2 ¾
		113	—
X	If man's blanket carried - add	5	8
	Grand Total	118	8

P.T.O.

Ø/ The method of carrying these articles dependent on whether regiments carry rifles on off or near side.

X Carried in 'B' echelon unless otherwise ordered.

....

MARCHING ORDER (Scale 'B')
―――――――――――――――――――――――

In Wallets .... 2 Iron Rations

In 2 Nosebags, or in)
Nosebag and cornsack)   ....   16 lbs Oats.

Signed
Brigade Major.

SERIAL NO. 111.

Confidential
War Diary
of

Headquarters Lucknow Cavalry Brigade

FROM 1st July 1916 TO 31st July 1916.

Army Form C. 2118.

WAR DIARY LUCKNOW CAV BDE.
or
INTELLIGENCE SUMMARY.

(Erase heading not required.)

Instructions regarding War Diaries and Intelligence Summaries are contained in F. S. Regs., Part II, and the Staff Manual respectively. Title page will be prepared in manuscript.

Hour, Date, Place.	Summary of Events and Information.	Remarks and references to Appendices
July 1st GROUCHES	Brigade put on 2½ hours notice to move, from time of receipt of orders at Brigade H.Q.	
" 2nd "	The Brigade received orders at 4.30pm to move to a new area & at 6.30pm marched via HAUTE VISÉE - RANSART + BARLY to billets as follows:— B.H.Q. M.u.S M.G.S & K.D.G.s FROHEN-LE-GRAND. 29th & 36th VILLERS L'HOPITAL.	
" 4th FROHEN LE GRAND	Division put at 8 hours notice to move.	
" 16th "	Division moved to be ready to move.	
" 18th "	"U" Battery left for Etrehem(?) to 4th Army	
" 19th "	Brigade marched in four attached orders & moved into billets as follows B.H.Q. 38th J.H M.u.S. VILLERS BRULIN - M.G.S BERTENCOURT - K.D.G.s 29th CAMBLIGNEUL. The Brigade was put under orders of 6th Bgde.	APPENDIX "A"
" 20th VILLERS BRULIN	In accordance with attached orders 300 men K.D.G. under Capt WIENHOLT moved up to MT ST ELOY. They were there led back & at 9pm. they marched to NEVILLE ST VAAST 7 men killed & more wounded the	" "B"

Army Form C. 2118.

WAR DIARY
or
INTELLIGENCE SUMMARY.

(Erase heading not required.)

LUCKNOW CAV. Bde.

Instructions regarding War Diaries and Intelligence Summaries are contained in F.S. Regs., Part II, and the Staff Manual respectively. Title pages will be prepared in manuscript.

Hour, Date, Place.	Summary of Events and Information.	Remarks and references to Appendices
Feb 20th VILLERS BRULIN	Orders of 180th Inf. Bde. for work under the 175th Tunnelling Coy. for work in O Sector. In event of attack they were placed under orders of O.C. NEWVILLE ST VAAST Defences. 300 men 2/5 Hrs. under Col CHEYNE. 300 38th under Capt FARQUHAR & 100 Jodhpur Lrs under Maj STRONG to be marched to MAROEUIL. Their horses were sent back & they billeted there the nights 20/21.	APPENDIX "D"
" 21st	The 2/5 Hrs. & Jodhpur parties marched at 6 a.m. to AUX RIETZ. Troops placed under the orders of 179th Bde for work under O.C. 181st Tunnelling Coy in N Sector. They were billeted in AUX RIETZ Cave & in event of attack were in Brigade reserve at AUX RIETZ. The 38th party were placed under orders of 181st Bde for work under O.C. 185th Tunnelling Coy in L T.M. Sector. Half were billeted in ABRI CENTRAL & were in L T in event of attack were under orders of O.C. "A" Regt. The remainder stayed in MAROEUIL, worked in M.T. & in event of attack were in Brigade Reserve.	

Army Form C. 2118.

WAR DIARY
of LUCKNOW CAV. BDE.
or
INTELLIGENCE SUMMARY.
(Erase heading not required.)

Instructions regarding War Diaries and Intelligence Summaries are contained in F.S. Regs., Part II, and the Staff Manual respectively. Title page will be prepared in manuscript.

Hour, Date, Place.	Summary of Events and Information.	Remarks and references to Appendices
AUX RIETZ July 21st	3 O.R. Jodhpur Lancers wounded.	
" 22nd	Killed 1 O.R. wounded 2 O.R. Jodhpur Lancers	
NEUVILLE ST VAAST "	Wounded 1 O.R. K.D.G.s	
ROCLINCOURT 23rd	Wounded 3 O.R. Jacob's Horse	
VILLERS BRULIN 24th	1 N.C.O. 7th Jaipur per Regt were attached to 179th 188th 176th Bdes. Units also assisted infantry with patrols.	
NEUVILLE ST VAAST 28th	1 O.R. K.D.G. wounded	
ROCLINCOURT "	1 O.R. 36th Killed	
" 27th	" " wounded	
VILLERS BRULIN 30th	The digging parties were relieved by Mhow Bde. K.D.G.s were relieved by Inniskillings – 24th by 2nd Lancers – 28th by C.I.H. The Jodhpur Lancers were relieved by 100 men from the same Regt. Reliefs were carried out according to orders. Task started 9 was completed at 9.0 AM 31st.	APPENDIX "C"
CHELERS 31st	Brigade H.Q. moved to CHELERS.	Ainsworth Major Brigade Major

SECRET.   No. G-64.   Headquarters 1st Indian Cavalry Division,
                                                        18th July 1916.

1. The Division will march to new area tomorrow, 19th instant, as
   follows:-

   SIALKOT Bde.-   To VI Corps Area.
                   Route - NEUVILLETTE, REBREUVIETTE, AMBRINES, IZEL-LES-
                           HAMEAU. Not to enter REBREUVIETTE till 11.0.
                           a.m. and to be clear of REBREUVIETTE by
                           12.30. p.m.

   LUCKNOW Bde.-   To XVII Corps Area about VILLERS-CHATEL.
                   Route - BONNIERES, REBREUVIETTE, AMBRINES, SAVY.
                           To reach REBREUVIETTE at 12.0. noon
                           and to be clear by 1.30. p.m.

   DIVL. TROOPS (in order named).   - Commander - Lieut-Colonel
   1ST IND. R.H.A. BDE (less "U" Bty).   HOLDEN, 5th Cavalry.
   FIELD SQDN.   Starting Point - Church in
   DIVL. HEADQRS.   VILLERS L'HOPITAL - 10.0. a.m.
   SIGNAL SQDN.   and to be clear of AUXI-LE-
   JODHPUR LANCERS.   CHATEAU by 9.0. a.m.
   FIELD AMBLCES (less Motor   Route - BONNIERES, REBREUVIETTE,
        Vehicles).   AMBRINES, SAVY whence they
                                                disperse to billets.

   "B" ECHELON, DIVL. TROOPS - In order of units will march under
                               orders of O.C.A.S.C. in rear of FIELD
                               AMBULANCES (less Motor Vehicles) -
                               Commander - Lieut. NEWINGTON, A.S.C.

   MHOW Bde.-   To billets about ST MICHEL-SUR-TERNOISE and
                           ROELLECOURT (East of ST POL).
                   Route - Main AUXI-LE-CHATEAU - ST POL road. Not
                           to enter AUXI-LE-CHATEAU till 9.0. a.m. and
                           to use roads South of R. AUTHIE only.
   AUX. H.T. COMPANY.- Will follow MHOW Bde as far as ST POL.

   MOTOR VEHICLES of FIELD AMBLCES.)
   DIVL. AMMN. PARK.   ) will move at 2.0. p.m.

   DIVL. SUPPLY COLUMN - Will move under orders of O.C.A.S.C.

   Fighting troops of Brigades and Divl. Troops may pass "B" Echelon of
   the Brigades in front. The latter will halt whilst being passed.

2. O.C. SIGNAL SQDN will detail one Motor Cyclist Despatch Rider to
   report to O.C. DIVL. TROOPS at Starting Point for duty during the march.

3. Divisional Report Centre will close at AUXI-LE-CHATEAU at 10.0. a.m.
   and open at VILLERS-CHATEL at same hour.

                                       C.A.C. Godwin
                                              General Staff,
                                       1st Indian Cavalry Division.

Sialkot Bde.   Jodhpur Lancers.   D.A.D.O.S.
Mhow   "   A.D.M.S.   Camp Comdt.   VI Corps.
Lucknow "   O.C.A.S.C.   A.P.M.   XVII Corps.
1st Ind. R.H.A. Bde. A.D.V.S.   French Mission
Field Sqdn.   Signal Sqdn.   Third Army.

SECRET. No. B.M. 289.

Headquarters,
Lucknow Cavalry Brigade.
18th July, 1916.

To,
    O.C., K.D.Gds.   Sig Troop.
           29th Lrs.   A.D.C.
           36th J.H.   B.S.O.
           M.G.S.   B.T.O.
           M.V.S.   B.V.O.

1.   The Brigade will march to VII Corps Area about VILLERS - CHATEL tomorrow.
       ROUTE,   BONNIERES - REBREUVIETTE - AMBRINES - SAVY.

Units (with 'A' echelon) will march independently and will be clear of VILLERS L'HOPITAL by following hours :-

        B.H.Q. and Sig Troop   9.0 a.m.
        29th Lrs.   9.15 a.m.
        36th J.H.   9.30 a.m.
        K.D.Gds.   9.45 a.m.
        M.G.S.   10.0 a.m.

Fighting troops will pass 'B' echelon ~~at ANCRE~~ and will not enter REBREUVIETTE before 12 noon.
All troops, including 'B' echelon will be clear of REBREUVIETTE by 1.30 p.m.

2.   'B' echelon (under B.T.O.) will march at 9.0 a.m., Starting Point, fork roads ¾ mile S.W. BONNIERES,-

       Order of march :-   29th Lrs.
                                     36th J.H.
                                     B.H.Q.
                                     K.D.Gds.
                                     M.G.S.
                                     M.V.S.

It will not enter REBREUVIETTE until all fighting troops have passed.

3.   Units will water as follows :-

        Sig Troop   )
        29th Lrs.   )   WAMIN.
        36th J.H.   ROZIERE.
        K.D.Gds.   BRONILLY.
        M.G.S.   REBREUVIETTE.
        'B' echelon   " "

4.   Fighting troops may pass 'B' echelon of Brigades in front.

5.   Billeting areas allotted to units will be notified later.

6.   Report centre will close at FROHEN LE GRAND at 10.0 a.m. and open at CAMBLIGNEUL at same hour.
       VILLERS BRULIN

                                                        Major,
Brigade Major, Lucknow Cavalry Brigade.

Copy of Q-2216 dated 18-7-16 from 1st Ind Cavalry Division.
****

ADMINISTRATIVE INSTRUCTIONS Issued in accordance with O-64.
****

1. The billeting areas will be as follows :-
Divisional Headquarters..............................(VILLERS CHATEL.
                                                      (MINGOVAL.
Jodhpur Lancers.................................... BETHONSART & GOUNETREVILLE.
R.H.A.Brigade,(less R.A.A.Section of B.A.C..)   ACQ & ECOIVRES. Same billets
~~///////////~~   as before.
R.A.A. Seen B.A.C. .... SAVY.
Divnl Amm Park..................................... SAVY
Field Squadron..................................... AGNIERES, Just North of MINGNY
Cav Fd Ambulances.................................. One at ECOIVRES, remainder
                                                      in TINCQUES.
Sanitary Section................................... TINCQUES.
Divnl Supply Column................................ TINCQUES.
A.H.T.Company...................................... GAUCHINY VERLOINCT, west of
                                                      ST POL.
Reserve Park....................................... Remain at BONDUES.
Mhow Brigade....................................... ST MICHEL - SUR - TERNOISE;
                                                      GRAND CAMPS ; HOLCOURT ST
                                                      LAMBERT; BOULLENCOURT.
Sialkot Brigade.................................... In the valley of R.CE. Area
                                                      will be given later.
Lucknow Brigade
Brigade Headquarters, advanced,.................... ECOIVRES.
Brigade Area....................................... VILLERS CAMBLIGNEUIL and
                                                      VILLERS BRULIN and BERLETTE.

   Troops already in these billets are not to be moved. Details
are sent herewith to those concerned.
2.   Divisional Headquarters will water at VILLERS CAMBLIGNEUIL. Jodhpur
Lancers will water at troughs South of main road between TINCQUES & BAILES.
3.   O.C.Field Squadron will obtain some extra water troughs from C.E.
XVII Corps.
4.   Staff Captain of Lucknow Brigade and billeting officers of Field Sqdn,
D.A.P. and R.A.C. will meet a Divisional Staff Officer at SAVY Railway
Station at 10 a.m. 19th.
5.   There are 127 tents pitched on rising ground at ST MICHEL on South
side of ST POL - ARRAS main road. These are available for the MHOW Brigade
and will be taken over there from A.D.G.S. XVII Corps.
6.   Railhead opens at TINCQUES on 20th.
7.   All units will send back two men today, on the empty supply lorries
to accompany the Supply Column tomorrow and take charge of dumped rations
at the new billets.
8.   Orders for the move of the D.H. will follow. They will rejoin their
units in the new billets.
9.   Ordnance and postal lorries will move with the Supply Column Hqrs.

No. G-63.

SECRET.

Headquarters,
1st Indian Cavalry Division.
18th July 1916.

MEMORANDUM.

1. The 1st Indian R.H.A. Brigade and Field Squadron are placed at the disposal of the 60th Division.
   The Officers Commanding these units will report at 60th Divl. HdQrs tomorrow, 19th instant, at 11.0. a.m.

2. LUCKNOW Brigade will supply a dismounted trench party of 900 men exclusive of the proper proportion of British Officers.

   The JODHPUR LANCERS will supply 100 dismounted men who will be attached to LUCKNOW Brigade.

   A proportion of Machine Guns and Hotchkiss Rifles will also be provided — numbers of these required to be ascertained from 60th Divn

   This detachment will be commanded by the Brigadier Commanding the Brigade and will proceed under Brigade arrangements on the 20th inst as under.—

   ADV. BDE. HDQRS. .... ECOIVRES.
   K.D.G'S. .... MONT ST ELOY.
   29th LANCERS.   )
   36th HORSE.   ) .... MAROEUIL.
   JODHPUR LANCERS.)

3. A Staff Officer from LUCKNOW Brigade will report at 60th Division HeadQrs tomorrow at 11.0.a.m. to receive instructions regarding duties and other details.

C. A. C. Godwin
Lieut-Colonel,
General Staff, 1st Indian Cavalry Division.

Lucknow Bde,
1st Ind. R.H.A. Bde.
Field Sqdn.
Jodhpur Lancers.
O.C.A.S.C.
"Q".
O.C. Signal Sqdn.
Third Army.
60th Division.
XVII Corps.
Town Major, NEUVILLE ST VAAST.
  "   "   MAROEUIL.
180th Infy. Bde.

SECRET. No. G-46. Headquarters 1st Indian Cavalry Division
18th July 1916.

In continuation of my No. G-65, paragraph 2.

a. The British Personnel will arrive at MONT ST ELOY by 4.0.p.m. and the Indian Personnel at same hour at MAROEUIL.

b. Billeting parties will report to Town Majors of NEUVILLE ST VAAST and MAROEUIL at 12.noon 20th July.

c. XVII Corps Cyclist Battalion are providing guides for billeting party of K.D.G's at BRUNEHAUT FARM (F.22.d) at 11.0.a.m. 20th July, and for the Regiment at HeadQrs 180th Infantry Brigade at MONT ST ELOY at 9.0.p.m.

C.A.C. Godwin
Lieut-Colonel,
General Staff, 1st Indian Cavalry Division.

Lucknow Bde.
Jodhpur Lancers.
O.C.A.S.C.
"Q".
Signal Sqdn.
Third Army.
60th Divn.
XVII Corps.
Town Major, NEUVILLE ST VAAST.
    "   "   MAROEUIL.
180th Infy. Bde.

Copy of a memo No. G-65 SECRET dated 18-7-16 from 1st I.C.Div.
....

1. The 1st Indian R.H.A. Brigade and Field Squadron are placed at the disposal of the 60th Division.
The Officers Comdg these units will report at 60th Divnl Hdqrs tomorrow 19th instant, at 11 a.m.

2. LUCKNOW Brigade will supply a dismounted trench party of 900 men exclusive of the proper proportion of British officers.

The Jodhpur Lancers will supply 100 dismounted men who will be attached to LUCKNOW Brigade.

A proportion of Machine Guns and Hotchkiss Rifles will also be provided - numbers of these required to be ascertained from 60th Div.

This detachment will be commanded by the Brigadier Commanding the Brigade, and will proceed under Brigade arrangements on the 20th inst as under :-

```
        ADV. BDE HQRS............ECOIVRES.
        K.D.GDS..................MONT ST ELOY.
        29TH LANCERS  )
        36TH J.HORSE  )..........MAROEUIL.
        JODHPUR LRS   )
```

3. A Staff officer from Lucknow Brigade will report at 60th Division Headquarters tomorrow at 11-0 a.m. to receive instructions regarding duties and other details.
....

Copy of a memo No. G-66 SECRET dated 18-7-16 from 1st I.C.Div.
....

In continuation of my No. G-65, paragraph 2.

a. The British personnel will arrive at MONT ST ELOY by 4-0 p.m. and the Indian personnel at same hour at MAROEUIL.

b. Billeting parties will report to Town Majors of NEUVILLE ST VAAST and MAROEUIL at 12 noon 20th July.

C/. XVII Corps Cyclist Battalion are providing guides for billeting party of K.D.Gds at BRUNEHAUT Farm (F.22 d.) at 11-0 a.m. 29th July, and for the regiment at Hqrs 180th Infantry Brigade at MONT ST ELOY at 9-0 p.m.

"A" Form.   Army Form C. 2121.

MESSAGES AND SIGNALS.

TO: Lucknow Bde
Jodhpur Lancers

Sender's Number: G.A.285
Day of Month: 19.7.16
AAA

In continuation my G 66 of 18". The 60' Division will arrange a conference of representatives of Regts supplying working parties and of Tunnelling Coys at AUX RIETZ at 3pm the 20° July. The XVII Cyclists Corps will provide guides at 2pm at BRUNEHAUT Farm to conduct above representatives. These representatives will consist of one Officer from the Lucknow Bde Staff and one Officer from the K.D.Y's, 29 Lrs, 36 Horse and Jodhpur Lancers.

From Place Time: 1st Ind: Cav: Division

(Z) Anderson Lt Col

"A" Form.
Army Form C. 2121.

MESSAGES AND SIGNALS.

No. of Message_____

Prefix____Code____m.	Words	Charge	This message is on a/c of:	Recd. at_____m.
Office of Origin and Service Instructions.				Date_____
	Sent			From_____
_____	At_____m.		_____Service.	
_____	To_____			_____
_____	By_____		(Signature of "Franking Officer.")	By_____

TO { OC, KDG.

Sender's Number.	Day of Month	In reply to Number	
* BM.298	19		AAA

1 Rif Div No G66 your working party of 300 men, with officers in proportion, will march mounted to MONT ST ELOY tomorrow afternoon arriving there 4-0 pm. at 9-0 pm. a guide will be provided at HQ. 180th Bde MONT ST ELOY to guide them to NEUVILLE ST VAAST where they will be billeted. No A.Rs, bombs or trench stores will be taken. Each man will carry 90 rds ammunition.

2. Billeting parties for above will meet a guide at BRUNEHAUT Fm (cross rds ½ m. N of M^n MARDEUIL) at 11.0 am; they can ride to MARDEUIL via ACQ-ECOIVRES - M^n de BRAY & along new road by river.

3. O.C. working party will meet Brigade Major at BRUNEHAUT Fm at 2-0 pm. to go to AUX RIETZ for conference with OC Tunnelling Coys when tasks will be allotted.

4. O.C. party will receive his orders for

From
Place
Time

The above may be forwarded as now corrected. (Z)

Censor. Signature of Addressor or person authorised to telegraph in his name.

* This line should be erased if not required.

"A" Form.
MESSAGES AND SIGNALS.

Army Form C. 2121.

dispositions in case of attack from O.C Sector NEUVILLE ST VAAST

The party remains under Brigade for administration.

5. Communication by phone to Advd B.H.Q. ECOIVRES.

6. Ref para 1 party should proceed a troop at a time, no horses to enter MONT ST ELOY.

From: B.M.

"A" Form.   Army Form C. 2121.
MESSAGES AND SIGNALS.   No. of Message_____

Prefix____Code____m.	Words	Charge	This message is on a/c of:	Recd. at____m.
Office of Origin and Service Instructions.				Date_____
	Sent		Service.	From_____
	At____m.			
	To____			By_____
	By____	(Signature of "Franking Officer.")		

TO { O.C. 29th L TO
     " 36th J.H.
     Jodh [?] TO

Sender's Number: B.M. 297
Day of Month: 19/7/16
In reply to Number:
AAA

1. Ref Div N° G 65 + 66 the working parties will rendezvous at N.W. exit of ACQ. If lorries cannot be provided they may ride down, proceeding a troop at a time. NO A.R.s bombs or trench stores will be taken. Each man will carry 90 rds ammunition.

2. Billeting parties as in G 66.

3. O.C. each regtl party will meet the B.M at BRUNEHAUT Fm (cross rds ½ m N of M in MAROEUIL) at 11-0 a.m. They can ride to MAROEUIL via ACQ - ECOIVRES - Mn de BRAY - along new road by river.

4. The senior officer will be in command of the Indian party & will receive his orders for dispositions in case of attack from O.C. Sector.
The party remains under Brigade for

From_____
Place_____
Time_____

The above may be forwarded as now corrected.   (Z)

Censor.   Signature of Addressor or person authorised to telegraph in his name.
* This line should be erased if not required.

"A" Form.
MESSAGES AND SIGNALS.
Army Form C. 2121.

administration.

5. Orders for working parties will be given to O.C's units at a conference with O.C Tunnelling Coys at AUX RIETZ 3 p.m. 20th (rendezvous as in para 3)

6. Billeting parties may ride to MARŒUIL by above route.

7. Communication by phone to Advd B.H.Q. ECOIVRES thence by D.R. to B.H.Q.

From B.M.

Major.

"A" Form.
MESSAGES AND SIGNALS.
Army Form C. 2121.

TO O.C. 29L
36th
I.L.

Sender's Number: Bm. 360
Day of Month: 19th
AAA

Ref Bm. 297 para 1.

If lorries are not provided troops may ride via the SAVY ARRAS main road and dismount immediately West of the 100 Contour map 1/100,000 which crosses the road 1500x NW of the E of ETRUN, from there they must march to MAROEUIL a troop at a time, 100x intervals between troops.

No. G-131.

SECRET.   Headquarters 1st Indian Cavalry Division,
25th July 1916.

Sialkot Bde.
Lucknow "
Jodhpur Lancers.
Signal Sqdn.
O.C.A.S.C.
A.D.M.S.
"Q"
Third Army.
XVIIth Corps.
60th Division.

Reference G-45, dated 18/7/16.

1. The SIALKOT Brigade will relieve the LUCKNOW Brigade Working Parties in 60th Division trenches on the 30th/31st.

2. The JODHPUR LANCERS will relieve their working party at the same time.

3. All arrangements for relief will be made direct between the Brigadiers concerned, who will include the JODHPUR LANCERS in their orders.

4. The reliefs must be so arranged that there is no cessation of work.

5. Completion of reliefs will be reported to Divisional HeadQrs.

Lieut-Colonel,
General Staff, 1st Indian Cavalry Division.

Copy to units & digging parties. B50 B70
Orders for relief will issue later.

UNIT.	TACTICAL. In event of attack.	WORK.	BILLETS	RATIONS.
F.D.Ss	Under 180th Brigade. Men working are placed under nearest Company Commander. Collected by Officer on duty and rejoin to take over section N. St V. Defences already allotted. Men in billets are allotted positions under O.C., NEUVILLE St VAAST defences.	Under O.C. 175th Tunnelling Company for work in O Sector.	NEUVILLE St VAAST.	By limber to reach MT St ELOY railway crossing 7.0 p.m. thence by truck to AUX RIETZ. Trucks to be ordered from R.T.O. ECOIVRES before 1.0 p.m. Water in NEUVILLE St VAAST.
29th Lrs. (50) Jod.Lrs. (100)	Under 180th Brigade. Men working as above. Men in billets remain in Brigade reserve.	Under O.C. 181st Tunnelling Company for work in N. Sector.	AUX RIETZ Cave. Offrs in NEUVILLE St VAAST.	As above. 2 water carts required - filled from R. SCARPE in MAROEUIL, goes up from there 9.30 each night to AUX RIETZ. Men can also draw from NEUVILLE St VAAST.
36th J.H. (300)	Under 181st Brigade. (a) Party 140 - working parties as above. Remainder under O.C., 'A' Regt. Under 179th Brigade. (b) Party 150 - working parties as above. Remainder in Brigade reserve MAROEUIL	Under O.C. 185th Tunnelling Company for work in L and M. Sector	(a) Party, half in ABRI CENTRALE, remainder in dug-outs near Bn H.Q. 'A' Regt. SABLIERS. (b) Party, MAROEUIL.	By limbers to MAROEUIL by day - Limber for (b) party leaves MAROEUIL after dark to dump near ARIANE. Water near Bn H.Q. and MAROEUIL.

King's Dragoon Guards.

1. **Billets.**

   'A' Squadron.
   No. of billet.
   - F 6 — 9 men.
   - F 8 — 10 "
   - E17 — 11 "
   - E18 — 22 "
   - E19 — 14 "
   - E14 — 6 "
   -       72.

   'B' Squadron.
   No. of billet.
   - A10 — 7 men.
   - A11 — 7 "
   - A12 — 7 "
   - A13 — 3 "
   - D 5 — 6 "
   - D 6 — 4 "
   - F 1 — 11 "
   - F 2 — 10 "
   - F 3 — 12 "
   - F 4 — 11 "
   - C 7 — 2 "
   -       80.

   'C' Squadron.
   No. of billet.
   - F 10a — 1 man.
   - F 10 — 3 men.
   - F 11 — 5 "
   - F 12 — 2 "
   - F 13 — 6 "
   - L 16 — 8 "
   - L 11 — 13 "
   - L 10 — 10 "
   - L 9   — 12 "
   - L 8   — 8 "
   - L 16 — 8 "
   - L 15 — 4 "
   -       80.

   'D' Squadron.
   No. of billet.
   - A 4 — 3 men.
   - C 4 — 13 "
   - C 6 — 12 "
   - C 7 — 3 "
   - C 9 — 5 "
   - C10 — 8 "
   - C13 — 2 "
   - C14 — 1 man.
   - C15a — 5 men.
   - D 2 — 6 "
   - D 3 — 9 "
   - D 4 — 9 "
   -       76.

2. **Tactical Dispositions.**

   'D' Squadron.
   From area A, C, and D assemble at Ration Dump. Proceed along PARALLEL VI - PIONEER DUMP - MONMOUTH STREET.

   'B' Squadron.
   From area A, D, and F, C, assemble at R.E. Dump. Proceed along SAPPER Road.

   'C' Squadron
   From area L and F, assemble at K.D.Gs advanced H.Q. Proceed along PARALLEL VIII.

   'A' Squadron.
   From area E and F, assemble in area E and proceed by troops to places allotted.

3. **Shifts.**
   No. of men employed on shifts from 70 to 80 varies daily.

   8 hours shifts.
   - 6.0 a.m.
   - 2.0 p.m.
   - 10.0 p.m.

   NOTE.
   The trenches marked on map are, in many places wrong. They have been corrected as far as they effect the K.D.Gds. Most of the Wells are incorrectly marked.

29th Lrs Digging Party.

(1) Men are billeted in AUX RIETZ Cavern.
    Officers in Billet No. N.16.

(2) In the event of attack, parties in the saps are conducted by the sapper in whose charge they are working to the nearest Company Commander and placed under his command for disposal as he considers necessary.
    Those in the Cavern will stand to and await orders.

(3) Number of men and hours of shifts :-

    100 men 5-30 a.m. - 1-30 p.m.
    150 " 9-30 p.m. - 5-0 a.m.

In point of fact the men usually return about 11-30 a.m. and 4-0 a.m., as they are on "piece work".

36th J. Horse Digging Party.

1. **Billets.**
    This party is divided into two parts –
    a. H.Q. and 2 squadrons at L'ABRI CENTRAL and L'ABRI SABLIER in the trenches.
    b. 2 squadrons at MAROEUIL.

2. **Party A.**
    Billets.
    a. One squadron is in a dug-out at L'ABRI CENTRAL.
    b. One squadron is in 3 dug-outs at L'ABRI SABLIER.
    c. Officers. Two at L'ABRI CENTRAL and two at SABLIER. As there is no place where they can mess together two are living with the Tunnelling Coy at SABLIER, one with the Battn H.Q., one with the Company at CENTRAL.

    ii. **Tactical Dispositions – Party A.**
    This party comes under the direct orders of the O.C. the Battn at SABLIER. He has allotted certain posts to be held by the men who are resting. Squadrons fall in at once and are taken to these posts.
    The procedure is the same in case of either an attack or gas attack.
    The men working are to do as the miners do, that is, stay in the shafts and then when the communication trenches are clear retire to the ABRI CENTRAL whence they will rejoin their squadron at their alarm posts.
    The gas alarm is sounded by mechanical horns and beating of gongs. There is a sentry posted by each squadron to help warn the men in the dug-outs.

    iii. **Working Parties.**
    The parties work in 3 reliefs of 8 hours
    from 4-0 a.m. to 12 noon
    12 noon to 8 p.m.
    8 p.m. to 4 a.m.
    Parties parade at SABLIER 15 minutes before the time to commence work, where the miners take them over.
    The two day shifts consist of 18 men from each squadron.
    The night shift of 20 men from each squadron.
    In addition the following parties are found.
    A ration party of 1 N.C.O. and 6 men from each squadron. This party leaves the SABLIER about 11 p.m. each night for LILLE Dump.
    Water pumping parties.
    The squadron at CENTRAL supplies one of 1 N.C.O. & 5 men which pumps from 6-30 a.m. to 8-30 a.m.
    The squadron at SABLIER one of 1 N.C.O. & 9 men which pumps from 6-8 p.m.

    iv. **Communication.**
    Each squadron has a man night and day at ANZIN Church to bring up any messages from MAROEUIL.

    v. **Water and Rations.**
    Water is drawn from tanks
    at CENTRAL between any hour
    SABLIER " 7-8 morning and evening.
    Rations come up on the L.G.S. Wagons to the LILLE Dump. Leave MAROEUIL 9-45 p.m. for the Brigade rendezvous at Y roads LUCHEUX at 10 p.m.
    The chuppatties are made at MAROEUIL and sent up – the meat and vegetables are cooked in the trenches.

- 2 -

3. **Party B.**

    Billetted in MAROEUIL.

    i. Officers No. 14 Bridge Street.
    I.O's and Men) 5 Church Street
) 5 Saint Eloy
)10 Church Street.

    ii. **Tactical Dispositions. - Party B.**
    The Squadrons in MAROEUIL with the exception of the men actually working now come under the 179th Brigade (Centre Sector). Lieut Landale has gone to this Brigade Headquarters for orders, which will be sent you tomorrow.
    The men of these Squadrons actually working will come under the orders of the O.C. Left Sub Sector of the 181st Brigade and they have orders to act with the miners who have orders to rendezvous at the ARIANE dump as soon as possible if unable to do so to man nearest fire trench.
    These men will be next sent met by an officer at the ARIANE dump, who will get orders from O.C. Left Sub Sector 181st Brigade.

    iii. **Working Parties.**
    These Squadrons are formed into 4 parties of 16 men each (i.e. 32 men each relief) each shift of 8 hours.
    They report at the ARIANE dump at 6.15 a.m., 2.15 p.m., 9.45 p.m., 6.15 a.m.
    It takes each party an hour to march from MAROEUIL to the ARIANE dump and about another three quarters of an hour from there before they begin work.
    The 3rd Shift reaches the ARIANE dump at 9.45 p.m. instead of 10.15 p.m. so as to allow the 2nd relief to come back to MAROEUIL on the empty ration trucks which go up to the ARIANE dump.

    iv. ~~Each Squadron as~~
    Communication.
    Each Squadron has a man night and day at ANZIN Church to bring any messages from the trench party.

    NOTE.
    ABRI CENTRALE.

1. Not more than 2 British Officers, remainder should be at MAROEUIL.

2. Water supply arranged locally from pipes - a proportion of petrol tins useful.

3. Cooking should be done at MAROEUIL or ARIANE except cooking of meat which can be done on Braziers.

4. Latrines - Trench system in ground already allotted - Sweepers not necessary.

Jodhpur Lrs Digging Party.

1. **Billets.**   100 men in AUX RIETZ Cavern.
   Two officers in C.10 in NEUVILLE ST VAAST.
   One officer with Town Major NEUVILLE ST VAAST.

2. **Tactical Disposition.**
   In case of attack all men on fatigues in the saps are collected by the R.E. officer on duty and taken to the nearest Infantry Company Commander, who will make use of them as he thinks fit.
   All men in AUX RIETZ Cavern stand to and await orders.

3. **Shifts.**
   100 men from 1-30 p.m. to 7-30 p.m.
   Each party returns independently as soon as it finishes its allotted task.

S.S.O Jodhpur Lancers.

Your party will be relieved by another 100 men from your Regt on 29th inst.
1 officer & 8 men should go up morning of 29th. The relief with the limber, should ride up so as to reach MAROEUIL at 9.30pm. Outgoing party will ride horses back.

A.M. Turner Major B.M.

B.M.364
SECRET.
HEADQUARTERS
LUCKNOW CAV BDE.

1. Reliefs will take place in accordance with table attached

2. During the day units will keep to communication trenches. when crossing exposed places parties should proceed in small groups at 50 yards distance.

3. Units will hand over all maps to relieving parties.

4. O.C. K.D.Gs. will send one limbered wagon to Mt St Eloy at 9-30. p.m. 30th to proceed after dark to La TARGETTE.

O.C. 29th Lancers will send one limbered wagon to MAROEUIL.

9-30.p.m. 30th inst to proceed to after dark to

AUX-RIETZ.
O.C. 36th J.H. will send one limbered wagon to MAROEUIL.

2-0.p.m. 30th JULY.

SECRET.   TIME TABLE OF RELIEFS 29th July, 1916.

TIME.	UNIT.	RENDEZVOUS.	ROUTE.	REMARKS.
12 noon	2 Officers and 8 men Iniskillings. 2 Officers and 8 men 2nd Lancers.	BRUNEHAUT Fm. "	Proceed by Teritorial trench to NEUVILLE St VAAST and AUX RIETZ.	K.D.Gds and 28th Lrs arrange guides to meet.
	2 Officers and 8 men C.I.H.	36th H.Q. MAROEUIL		36th J.H. to guide to ABRI CENTRALE.
9.30 p.m.	100 J.Lrs	MAROEUIL	NEUVILLE St VAAST. MAROEUIL Road.	Take over horses of incoming party W. exit MAROEUIL. Not leave MAROEUIL till dark.
"	100 J.Lrs	AUX RIETZ	"	
			30th.	
10 a.m.	100 K.D.G	Leave by lorry from X roads near E. of ETRUN.	Teritorial trench – MAROEUIL.	
	100 Inniskillings.	Leave BRUNE-HAUT Fm.	Teritorial trench.	Inniskillings provide guide.
4 p.m.	160 29th Lrs.	Leave by Lorry from X roads E of ETRUN.	"	
4 p.m.	160 2nd Lrs.	Leave BRUNE-HAUT Fm.	"	2nd Lrs provide guide.
"	160 36th J.H.	Leave by Lorry from X roads E of ETRUN.		
"	160 C.I.H.	Take over 36th billets in MAROEUIL.		C.I.H. provide guide.
M.N. 12 Noon 30/31st	200 K.D.Gds	Leave by lorry from MAROEUIL	NEUVILLE St VAAST – MAROEUIL road.	
"	200 Inniskillings.	Leave MAROEUIL for NEUVILLE St VAAST.	"	Inniskillings provide guide.

30th.

TIME.	UNIT.	RENDEZVOUS.	ROUTE.	REMARKS.
4 p.m.	140 C.I.H.	Arrive MAROEUIL	Proceed by detachments via ANZIN to ABRI CENTRALE.	C.I.H. provide guide.
10 p.m.	140 36th J.H.	Leave by lorry MAROEUIL.	via GENIE Trench-Auzin.	
9 a.m.	140 9th Lrs.	Leave by lorry from E of ETRUN.	Teritor'al Trench and MAROEUIL.	
9. a.m.	140 2nd Lrs.	Leave BRUNEHAUT Fm.	Teritorial	2nd Lrs provide guide.

SERIAL NO. 111.

Confidential
War Diary
of

Headquarters, Lucknow Cavalry Brigade.

FROM 1st August 1916. TO 31st August 1916.

Army Form C. 2118.

WAR DIARY of LUCKNOW CAV. Bde.

INTELLIGENCE SUMMARY.

(Erase heading not required.)

Instructions regarding War Diaries and Intelligence Summaries are contained in F.S. Regs., Part II, and the Staff Manual respectively. Title page will be prepared in manuscript.

Hour, Date, Place.	Summary of Events and Information.	Remarks and references to Appendices
August 1st CHELERS.	The KDG's moved into billets at MONCHY BRETON The 29th Lancers to billets in CHELERS (H.Q.) GUESTREVILLE & LE TIRLET for Brigade Training with MONCHY BRETON area. One Squadron KDG's under Maj Spooner one Squadron 36th (Maj Davidson) the British Section of the London Squadron (Lt Ward) with 1 Company Artists Rifles & 3 Sections A.A. were detached/under the G.O.C., as escort to His Majesty during his stay at BRYAS' Château. The KDG Squadron also billeted in HERNICOURT & the 31st Squadron in GAUCHIN - the remainder at BRYAS.	
" 9th "	The Brigade under Lt Col Birkbeck KDG. marched via AVESNES to PAS for entrainment to VII Corps & was billeted as follows B.H.Q. PAS - KDG TinlotS HUMBERCOURT - 29th WARLINCOURT - 36th GUADIEMPRE	
" 10th PAS	The detached Squadrons KDG & 36th were inspected at BRYAS by his Majesty & rejoined their Units in VII Corps area	

Army Form C. 2118.

WAR DIARY
of
LUCKNOW CAV Bde
INTELLIGENCE SUMMARY.
(Erase heading not required.)

Instructions regarding War Diaries and Intelligence Summaries are contained in F.S. Regs., Part II, and the Staff Manual respectively. Title pages will be prepared in manuscript.

Hour, Date, Place.	Summary of Events and Information.	Remarks and references to Appendices
August 10th PAS	A working party of 7 British Officers 8 I.O.s & 365 O.R. 2/F Lancers & 6 Brit Officers, 8 I.O.s, 9 270 O.R. 3/F Horse, under Major Henderson 29/F Lancers moved (dismounted) up to trenches in SOUASTZ in accordance with orders attached for work number 56 E Div. They were employed on nights 10/11 - 11/12 & 12/13 in carrying up of gas cylinders to the front line trenches in front of FONQUEVILLERS. On completion of the work they rejoined their mounts in 13 S mor. The G.O.C. 57th Div expressed his appreciation of the way in which the work had been carried out. Casualties: - 36 E. 1 Killed 3 wounded - 29 E 1 O.R. wounded.	APPENDIX "A"
11th	A working party of 7 Officers & 250 O.R. K.D.Gs under Capt HARVEY K.D.Gs moved up dismounted to forward trenches in POMMIER for work number 46 E Div. They were employed in accordance with orders attached on carrying up of gas cylinders to the front line on the nights of 11th/12th 12th/13 & 13th/14th.	

WAR DIARY or **INTELLIGENCE SUMMARY.**

LUCKNOW CAV. Bde.

Army Form C. 2118.

(Erase heading not required.)

Instructions regarding War Diaries and Intelligence Summaries are contained in F. S. Regs., Part II, and the Staff Manual respectively. Title page will be prepared in manuscript.

Hour, Date, Place.	Summary of Events and Information.	Remarks and references to Appendices
August 14th PAS	The working party K.D.G.'s reported their went a completion of the work. Casualties 3 O.R. wounded.	
" 12th	Lt. Col. GORE resumed command of the Brigade & the detached Section M.G.S. rejoined their squadron.	
" 15th "	One B.O., one I.O. & 7 Sappers each of 24th & 36th were attached to 169th Infy Bde for patrol work.	Jhind escort Bde M.Gun 175th returned 5th Lrs.
" 16th "	One officer & 8 Sappers K.D.G. were attached to 137th F. Bde.	
" 18th "	" 4 Hotchkiss from detachment were attached to 139th Bde for duty.	
" 22nd "	A working party of 4 officers & 150 men K.D.G.'s proceeded to billets in SAILLY AU BOIS for work under the 175th Div. 121st Tunnelling Coy to supplement E/HASLETONS. A similar party of 36th Lancers were proceeded to billets in BIEN VILLERS for work under the same Company in Sap. E of FONQUEVILLERS. The K.D.G. party was commanded by CAPT STURRIER & the 36th by Major DAVIDSON.	

Army Form C. 2118.

LUCKNOW CAV. Bde

WAR DIARY
or
INTELLIGENCE SUMMARY.
(Erase heading not required.)

Instructions regarding War Diaries and Intelligence Summaries are contained in F. S. Regs., Part II, and the Staff Manual respectively. Title page will be prepared in manuscript.

Hour, Date, Place.	Summary of Events and Information.	Remarks and references to Appendices
Aug 23rd PAS	A working party of 125 men each of K.E.O.'s 29th and details for daily work entry shuttle in LUCKNOW was under the Corps Sappers.	
29th "	The 29th Lancers relieved the 38th / Central Horse working parties - the latter came out for 1 weeks work at Gouzy.	
31st "	Casualties during week ending 29th K.D.G. 2 OR wounded. No Change	

Antrooather
Brigade Major

"A" Form.
MESSAGES AND SIGNALS.
Army Form C. 2121.

SECRET

TO:
- 29ᵗʰ Lancers — Lucknow Cav F.A.
- 36ᵗʰ J. Horse
- Maj C.G.H. Henderson

Sender's Number	Day of Month	In reply to Number	AAA
BM 473	9.8.16		

(1) 29ᵗʰ Lancers 7 British Officers, 8 I.O's, 365 O.R.
36ᵗʰ J.H. 6   "   , 8 " , 270 "
Will march by road to SOUASTRE, on 10.8.16 timed to arrive at huts at D 22. C by 10 AM.

(2) One Officer per Regt. should report to Town Major SOUASTRE by 9.30 am, on 10.8.16.

(3) Major C.G. Henderson 29ᵗʰ Lancers will be in Command of the parties of both Regts after they arrive at SOUASTRE. He will issue all orders for working parties concerning which separate orders are being issued.

(4) Medical Officer 36ᵗʰ J. Horse will accompany party.

(5) Dismounted marching order 90 rounds in one bandolier. Baggage and rations may be sent up on transport at any time to SOUASTRE.

(6) Water from a well in hutted camp.

From: Copy No 1. Maj Henderson   4 Lucknow C+A.
Place: 2 29. L   5 167 Bde
Time: 3 36 JH

"A" Form.
MESSAGES AND SIGNALS.
Army Form C. 2121.

Prefix .... Code .... m.	Words	Charge	This message is on a/c of:	Recd. at .... m.
Office of Origin and Service Instructions.				Date ....
	Sent		.... Service.	From ....
	At .... m.			
	To			
	By		(Signature of "Franking Officer.")	By ....

TO — ②

| Sender's Number. | Day of Month. | In reply to Number. | A A A |

⑦ Sanitation — Special latrines have been dug these must be used and must be filled in before billets are vacated.

⑧ A Copy of Town Orders is being sent to Major Henderson for publication to all ranks.

⑨ Officers may take up horses.

⑩ Figures given in para 1, represent strength of working parties which will be required each night, all cooks, orderlies and batmen will be in excess of these numbers.

⑪ Casualties will be reported by Major Henderson to 167th Bde H.Q. by 9am. Nil returns should be submitted — Casualty returns will be repeated by Regiments to the Bde for information. — Code words given in 1st I.C.D., G-204 will be used.

⑫ Men of M.G.S. will not accompany working party.

From	Brigade	Major
Place	Lucknow	Cav Bde.
Time		

The above may be forwarded as now corrected.   (Z) Henshrd   C. ✓ Bde BM

Censor.   Signature of Addressor or person authorised to telegraph in his name.

* This line should be erased if not required.

"A" Form.
Army Form C. 2121.
MESSAGES AND SIGNALS.

Prefix Code m.	Words	Charge	This message is on a/c of:	Recd. at m.
Office of Origin and Service Instructions.				Date
	Sent		Service.	From
	At m.			
	To			
	By	(Signature of "Franking Officer.")	By

TO (3)

| Sender's Number. | Day of Month. | In reply to Number. | AAA |

(6) In all Telegraphic and Telephonic communications
O Cy 4th Bde Spec Bde = PICK.
Cylinders = PROPS

(7) Absolute Silence must prevail.

(8) Each Party will consist of 1 British Officer
4 Indian Officers or N.C.O.'s 60 men amongst
whom some N.C.O.'s will have to be
included vide para 3.

From Brigade Major
Place Lucknow Cav Bde.
Time

SECRET.   Copy No. 16

56th DIVISIONAL ORDER No. 21.   August 7th 1916.

1. "O" Company, 4th Battalion, Special Brigade moves to FONQUEVILLERS on the evening of the 9th instant.
   Headquarters of the Company will be temporarily established at Advanced Divisional Headquarters at SOUASTRE.

2. In all telegraphic or telephonic messages the following code words will be used:-

   "O" Coy., 4th Bn. Special Bde. = PICK.
   Cylinders   = PROPS.

3. On the nights of the 10/11th, 11/12th, 12/13th, some 1,600 cylinders will be placed in the specially prepared emplacements in "Y" and "Z" Sectors, in the mine shafts N. and S. of the FONQUEVILLERS - GOMMECOURT Road, and in the five shelters in Y.54/6, Y.55/1, Y.55/4, Y.56/1 and Y.56/5.

4. Cylinders will be conveyed to dumps at FONQUEVILLERS by lorry. Carrying parties will be provided to carry cylinders from the dumps to the emplacements. Three men will be detailed for each cylinder; this allows one spare, as the cylinders are slung from poles, which are carried on the shoulders of two men.

5. <u>Strength of parties</u>. Parties will consist of one officer, 4 N.C.O's and 60 men and each party will carry 20 cylinders.

6. Positions of dumps, routes to be followed, number of parties, times etc., are shown on attached Tables A and B.

7. Guides will be provided by "O" Company, Special Brigade to accompany parties to the emplacements.

8. <u>Equipment</u>. Every officer, N.C.O. and man with carrying parties will wear their smoke helmets in the alert position. N.C.O's and every third man will carry a rifle and bandolier. All men will carry a sandbag which will be folded to form a pad on the shoulder. The C.R.E. will arrange for an adequate supply of sandbags at the dumps.

9. All officers in command of carrying parties will reconnoitre their routes; 167th Brigade will arrange to provide guides to show the officers of the Lucknow Cavalry Brigade the routes allotted to them.

10. All carrying parties will report at the dumps to the officer of "O" Company, 4th Bn. Special Brigade, who will provide them with cards showing the number of the emplacement to which they are to proceed.
    Officers in command of carrying parties are responsible for returning all poles to the dumps, where they will obtain receipts from the officer of the Special Brigade.

/11.

11. Routes allotted in Table A are to be left clear for carrying parties from 10.0 pm. on all three nights. 167th and 169th Brigades will arrange for trench police to be stationed or blocks established at all trench junctions on these routes.

12. 167th Brigade will arrange for an exit to be made and a guide to be stationed at the point selected for carrying parties to leave trench and proceed by the "Z" road on return journey.

13. The importance of silence will be impressed on all ranks.

14. Acknowledge.

J. Brind

Head Qrs. 56th Divn.
7th August, 1916.

Lieut-Colonel,
General Staff.

Issued at 6.30 a.m. 8.8.16.

Copy Nos.

1. VIIth Corps
2. G.O.C. 56th Divn.
3. 167th Infantry Bde.
4. 168th   "   "
5. 169th   "   "
6. 5th Cheshires
7. C.R.A.
8. C.R.E.
9. A.D.M.S.
10. A.P.M.
11. Div. Signals.
12. War Diary
13. "G"
14. "Q"
15. "O" Coy. Sp. Bde. R.E.
16. Lucknow Cav. Bde.
17. Div. Gas Officer.

TABLE "A".

Issued with 56th Divisional Order No. 21.

POSITION of DUMPS and ROUTES.

Dump "A" Cross Roads at E.27.c.80.95.
(serves front line between FIFTH AVENUE and the GOMMECOURT ROAD)

Route A.1. IN THORPE STREET - FIFTH AVENUE - Left along fire trench.

OUT GOOCH STREET - Dump.

Route A.2. IN ST. MARTINS LANE - Right along fire trench.

OUT GOOCH STREET - Dump.

Route A.3. IN ST. MARTINS LANE - Left along fire trench.

OUT by the lower GOMMECOURT ROAD.

Dump "B". West end of CALVAIRE ROAD at E.27.b.40.70.
(serves front line between GOMMECOURT ROAD and the "Z" Road)

Route B.4. IN Dump - CALVAIRE ROAD - LINCOLN LANE - Right along fire trench.

OUT by the GOMMECOURT ROAD to the Dump.

Route B.5. IN LINCOLN LANE - Left along fire trench.

OUT by "Z" Road to the dump.

Dump "C" at W. end of COLONELS WALK at E.21.d.12.50.
(serves front line between "Z" Road and LA BRAYELLE ROAD.)

Route C.6. IN COLONELS WALK - SNIPERS SQUARE - ROBERTS AVENUE - Right along fire trench.

OUT by "Z" Road to the dump.

Route C.7. IN As before to ROBERTS AVENUE - Left along fire trench.

OUT ROBINSON LANE - LA BRAYELLE ROAD to the dump.

TABLE "B".
Issued with 56th Divisional Order No. 21.

Dates	Time	Brigade	No. of Parties	Offrs.	N.C.O's.	Men	Rendezvous	No. of cylinders to be carried.	Routes.
10th,11th,12th	10.0pm.	Lucknow Cavalry.Bde.	3	3	12	180	} Dump "A"	} 60 / 60 / 80	} A.1, A.2, A.3.
	10.30pm.	-do-	3	3	12	180			
	11.0pm.	-do-	4	4	16	240			
10th, 11th	10.0pm.	167th	3	3	12	180	} Dump "B"	} 60 / 60 / 80	} B.4, & B.5
	10.30 pm.	"	3	3	12	180			
	11 pm.	"	4	4	16	240			
10th, 11th	10 pm.	169th	3	3	12	180	} Dump "C"	} 60 / 60 / 80	} C.6 & C.7
	10.30 pm.	"	3	3	12	180			
	11 pm.	"	4	4	16	240			
12th		167th & 169th		Details later.					

SECRET.   Copy. No. 16

56th DIVISIONAL ORDER No. 22.   10.8.16.

1. On nights of 10/11th, 11/12th, 12/13th from 10 pm. until the carrying is completed, a Staff Officer will remain in touch with the Officer Commanding "O" Company, 4th Battalion, Special Brigade whose Headquarters will be at the SHRINE, FONQUEVILLERS. The Staff Officer will be provided, on the night

    10/11th by 56th Division.
    11/12th by 167th Brigade.
    12/13th by 169th Brigade.

    The operation is being carried out under the orders of the Officer Commanding "O" Company, Special Brigade, but in the event of any unforeseen circumstance arising, reference will be made to the Brigadier General Commanding 167th Brigade, who will decide on the action to be taken.

2. The following special precautions will be taken during the period the cylinders are in the trenches:-

    (a). Tube helmets will be worn in the Alert Position, in and East of FONQUEVILLERS, between Y.50 inclusive, and CRAWL BOY'S LANE.

    (b). Twenty additional Vermorel Sprayers are being issued to 167th Brigade and ten to 169th Brigade.

    (c). Brigades will ensure that there is an ample supply of solution in close proximity to all sprayers, and will ensure that blanket protection over doors of all dug-outs (which remain occupied) is satisfactory.

3. Acknowledge.

                                              J. Brind
Hdqrs. 56th Divn.   Lieut. Colonel,
10th August, 1916.   General Staff.

        Issued at 12 Noon, 10.8.16.

Copy Nos.

    1. VIIth Corps   10. A P.M.
    2. G.O.C., 56th Div.   11. Div. Signals.
    3. 167th Infantry Bde.   12. War Diary.
    4. 168th   "   "   13. "G"
    5. 169th   "   "   14. "Q"
    6. 5th Ches. Regt.   15. "O" Coy. Sp Bde R.E.
    7. C R.A.   16. Lucknow Cav. Bde.
    8. C. R. E.   17. Div. Gas Officer.
    9. A.D.M.S.

"A" Form.
MESSAGES AND SIGNALS.
Army Form C. 2121.
No. of Message............

Prefix.......... Code........... m.	Words	Charge	This message is on a/c of :	Recd. at.................m.
Office of Origin and Service Instructions.				
	Sent		............................Service.	Date....................
	At................ m.			
Secret	To.............			From Copy No 7.
	By.............		(Signature of "Franking Officer.")	By

TO	K D Gds	Lucknow Cav¹. Inf. Bde	
	138ᵗʰ Bde	Capᵗ Harvey	
	46ᵗʰ Divⁿ		

Sender's Number	Day of Month	In reply to Number	
* BM 679	10-8-'16		**AAA**

Ref Map 1/40000 and VII Corps Sketch 1/10000 No 192

(1) In accordance with 46ᵗʰ Divⁿ no 1878/G. the K D Gds. will furnish a working party, strength Officers 7 including medical Officer OR. 250 Capᵗ E. HARVEY will command the party

(2) Party under Capᵗ HARVEY will arrive in billets at POMMIER not later than 12 noon on 11ᵗʰ inst.

(3) Billeting party should report to Town Major POMMIER who has allotted billets.

(4) Rations will be sent up daily from HUMBERCOURT under Regimental arrangements

(5) Casualties to be reported to 138ᵗʰ Bde daily by 8 A.M. and repeated to Lucknow Bde for information Code words issued under 1ˢᵗ S.C.D 304 will be used

From
Place
Time

The above may be forwarded as now corrected.   (Z)

....
Censor.   Signature of Addressor or person authorised to telegraph in his name.

* This line should be erased if not required.
(A1) C. Ltd., London— W.14042/M.44. 150,000 Pads. 12/15. Form C.2121.

"A" Form.
MESSAGES AND SIGNALS.
Army Form C. 2121.

(6) Officers will meet a guide at 138" Bde HQ POMMIER who will point out the way to the routes to be used as laid down in appendix "A" of 46th Divn's O. 1878.

(7) The following sigint maps are issued. They will be returned to Lucknow Cav Bde HQ as soon as work is finished
VII Corps 1/10000   No 192   5 Copies

(8) Cap Harvey will report on arrival to 138" Infantry Bde at POMMIER.

Copy No			
1	KDG	5	138" Bde
2	Cap Harvey	6	46" Divn
3	Spare	7	Office
4	Lucknow CFA		

From Brigade Major Lucknow Cav Bde

"A" Form.   Army Form C. 2121.
MESSAGES AND SIGNALS   No. of Message............

Prefix...... Code......m.	Words	Charge	This message is on a/c of :	Recd. at............m.
Office of Origin and Service Instructions.				
	Sent		Service.	Date............
	At......m.			From
SECRET	To......			Copy No 5.
	By		(Signature of "Franking Officer.")	By

TO { K.D.Gds.   138th Bde.
     Capt Harvey
     46 Div

Sender's Number	Day of Month	In reply to Number	
BM 57	11. 7. 16		AAA

Ref. 46th Divn 1895/1.G and Appendix "A" Amended

(1) In order to bring the strength of the K.D.G. party at POMMIERS up to requirements for night of 13th Aug the following will be sent up to POMMIERS to arrive by 12 noon on 13th inst
               2 NCOs   16 privates

(2) Capt Harvey will please apply to 138th Bde direct for additional billeting accommodation

                    Copy No 1   46 Div
                         2   K.D.G.
                         3   Capt Harvey
                         4   138th Bde
                         5

From Brigade Major Lucknow Cav Bde
Place
Time

"A" Form.
Army Form C. 2121.
MESSAGES AND SIGNALS.
No. of Message ....

Prefix ....*.... Code .... m. Words Charge   This message is on a/c of: Recd. at .... m.
Office of Origin and Service Instructions.   Date ....
                                        Sent
                                                       .... Service.   From ....
      SECRET   At .... m.
                                     To
                                     By   (Signature of "Franking Officer.") By Copy N°3

TO { K.D.G.   138th Bde.
     Capt Harvey.
     46th Divn

Sender's Number.   Day of Month.   In reply to Number.
* B.M. 485   11.8.16   46th Dns G 791   A A A

Cont BM. 479.

Ref. Appendix "A" issued with 46th Divns 1878/G.

K.D. Gds. will supply party N° 16 on night of 12/13th Aug.

In order to supply this party K.D. Gds will send up on 12th inst to POMMIER the following 1 Officer 2 N.C.Os. 36 privates.

Capt Harvey will kindly apply to 138th Bde for additional billeting accommodation in POMMIER.

Copy N° 1 46th Dn   4 K.D.G.   7 Spare
         2 138th Bde   5 Cap Harvey
         3 File   6 Spare

From   Brigade Major Lucknow Cav. Bde.
Place
Time
    The above may be forwarded as now corrected.   (Z)   H. Beresford Capt for BM
                                Censor.   Signature of Addressee or person authorised to telegraph in his name.
* This line should be erased if not required.

S E C R E T.

46th Division.
1878/G.

137th Inf. Brigade.
138th   do.
139th   do.
Lucknow Cav. Brigade.
1/Monmouths.
O.C. 'P' Coy. Special Bde. R.E.

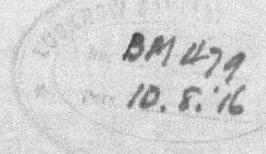

1.   The attached Appendix "A" gives the carrying parties which will be required for carrying on the nights of 11th/12th, 12th/13th and 13th/14th August.

2.   Times and places these parties are to report are shewn in Appendix 'A'. Also routes each party is to follow.

3.   Parties arriving at the rendezvous must be kept strictly to the side of the road to avoid interfering with lorry traffic.

4.   The parties are organised in two sub-parties. For each party one officer will be detailed and for each sub-party two N.C.Os. One N.C.O. marching in front of and one behind his sub-party. One R.E. guide will be provided for each sub-party.

5.   Carrying parties will not wear caps or steel helmets. They will wear gas helmets on their heads rolled up and the top button of their jackets undone.

6.   The rifles of men carrying cylinders will be carried by the third man.

7.   There must be no smoking and absolute silence will be kept up from the dump inclusive till the men have deposited their poles again at the pole dump.

8.   Poles must not be raised over the shoulder after the accessory has been dumped at its emplacement.

9.   Officers in charge of parties must keep their parties together and prevent any straggling and stop gaps occurring.

10.   If men are wounded on the way up, they must be lifted out of the Communication trenches. A block must not be allowed to occur.

11.   Should a cylinder be hit and burst, no gas alarm is to be sounded. Men will put their helmets down and the R.E. guide will be informed. On no account is the gas alarm to be sounded.

12.   Secrecy must be impressed on all men.

13.   There will be no traffic in the trenches detailed for the carrying operations and these trenches must be kept clear.

14.   On the way back, care must be taken to prevent noise walking along the MONCHY Road. Parties must keep on the sides of the road and avoid noise of tramping.

2.

15. Traffic Officers will be detailed as follows :-

Night 11th/12th and 12th/13th.

    RAVINE (end of NOBS WALK)
        One Officer from 137th Inf. Brigade.
    Head of NEWARK St.
        One officer from 137th Inf. Brigade.
    Head of NEVERENDING St.
        One officer from *138th Inf. Brigade.   * 137th
    Junction of NAKED St. with Support line.
        One officer 138th Inf. Brigade.
    Entrance into NAKED St.
        One officer 138th Inf. Brigade.
    Exit to MONCHY - BIENVILLERS Road.
        One Officer 138th Inf. Brigade.

Night of 13th/14th.

    Only Traffic officers as detailed by 138th Inf. Brigade for previous nights.
    Each Traffic officer will have 2 orderlies with him.

16. On arrival at emplacements for cylinders, cylinders will be dumped near the emplacement. The party will lead on, 4 men per sub-party being left to assist in putting the cylinders in the emplacement.

17. On conclusion of carrying operations all poles will be brought back to pole dump. These will be for BIENVILLERS at cross roads at Church.
    For BERLES at original dump for accessories.

                                                                  G. Thorpe

9th August, 1916.   Lieut-Col.,
                                                             General Staff, 46th Division.

Appendix. A.

Carrying Operations — Night of 11th/12th

Rendezvous BIENVILLERS. W.26.d.9.2.

No: of Party		Officers	N.C.Os	Other Ranks	Time to report	Load	Emplace: m:ed.	Route for all parties :— DUMP - NAKED ST turn right along support line and	Route out.	Unit furnishing Party
1	a	1	2	30	4 pm	10 cylinders	2 for 5 3 .. = 6	→ 90 Street	MONCHY- BIENVILLERS Road, or STONEYGATE STREET.	Lucknow Cav: Bde
	b		2	24		8	5	→ turn right		"
2	a	1	2	24	9.10	8	6	along front		"
	b		2	30		10	7	line.		"
3	a	1	2	30	9.20	10	8			"
	b		2	24		8	9			"
4	a	1	2	30	9.30	10	10	→ 91 Street		"
	b		2	30		10	12	→ turn right		"
5	a	1	2	30	9.40	10	13	along fire	"	138 ?: Bde
	b		2	30		10	14	trench.		"
6	a	1	2	30	9.50	10	15		"	"
	b		2	24		8	16			"
7	a	1	2	30	10.25	10	4	→ 90 Street	"	"
	b		2	24		8	5	→ turn right		"
8	a	1	2	24	10.35	8	6	along fire		"
	b		2	30		10	7	trench.	"	"
9	a	1	2	30	10.45	10	8		"	"
	b		2	24		8	9		"	"
10	a	1	2	30	10.55	10	10	→ 91 Street	"	"
	b		2	30		10	12	→ turn right	"	"
11	a	1	2	30	11.5	10	13	along fire	"	"
	b		2	30		10	14	trench.		"
12	a	1	2	30	11.15	10	15			"
	b		2	24		8	16		"	"
13	a	1	2	24	11.50	8	6	→ 90 Street	"	"
	b		2	30		10	7	→ turn right along fire trench.	"	"
14	a	1	2	30	12 m.n	10	8		"	"
	b		2	24		8	9	→ 91 Street	"	"
15	a	1	2	30	12.10 AM	10	10	→ turn right	"	"
	b		2	30		10	12	along	"	"
16	a	1	2	30	12.20	10	13	fire trench	"	"
	b		2	30		10	14		"	"
17	a	1	2	30	12.30	10	15	"	"	"
	b		2	24		8	16		"	"
18		1	2	30	1.5	10	7	→ 90 Street	"	"
19		1	2	30	1.10	10	8	→ 91 Street → turn right	"	"
20			2	30		10	15	along fire trench	"	"

348 cylinders

Carrying Operations, Night of 12th/13th

Rendezvous BIENVILLERS

Rendezvous BIENVILLERS. W.26.d.8.2.

No. of Party		Officers	N.C.Os	O.R.	Time to Report	Load	Emplacements	Route In (Route for all parties → NAKED ST. → Turn right along Support Line)	Route Out	Unit Furnishing Party
1	a	1	2	30	9 p.m	10 cylinders	20		NEVERENDING ST.	138th Bde
	b		2	30		10	19	→ 91 Street	→ RAVINE	do
2	a	1	2	24	9.10 pm	8	13	→ Turn Left along	→ DUMP	do
	b		2	30		10	14	Fire Trench		do
3	a	1	2	30	9.20 pm	10	8			do
	b		2	24		8	9			do
4	a	1	2	30	9.30 pm	10	10	→ 91 Street	84 Street and	do
	b		2	33		11	12	→ Turn RIGHT	STONEYGATE ST	do
5	a	1	2	30	9.40 pm	10	13	along Fire Trench	(or BIENVILLERS RD)	do
	b		2	30		10	14			do
6	a	1	2	30	9.50 pm	10	15			do
	b		2	24		8	16			do
7	a	1	2	30	10.24 pm	10	20			do
	b		2	30		10	19	→ 91 Street	NEVERENDING ST	do
8	a	1	2	24	10.26 pm	8	13	→ Turn LEFT	→ RAVINE → DUMP	do
	b		2	30		10	14	along Fire Trench		do
9	a	1	2	30	10.45 pm	10	8			do
	b		2	24		8	9			do
10	a	1	2	24	10.50 pm	8	11	→ 91 Street	84 Street and	do
	b		2	33		11	12	→ Turn RIGHT	STONEYGATE ST	do
11		1	2	36	11.5 pm	12	13	along Fire Trench	(or BIENVILLERS RD)	do
12	a	1	2	30	11.10 pm	10	15			do
	b		2	24		8	16			do
13	a	1	2	30	11.45 pm	10	20		NEVERENDING ST	Lucknow Coy Bde
	b		2	30		10	19	→ 91 Street	84 Street and	do
14	a	1	2	24	11.55 pm	8	18	→ Turn LEFT	STONEYGATE ST	do
	b		2	30		10	14	along Fire Trench	(or BIENVILLERS RD)	do
15	a	1	2	30	12.5 am	10	8			do
	b		2	24		8	11			do
⊗ 16		1	2	36	12.15 am	12	13			3rd do ⊗
17	a	1	2	30	12.20 am	10	15			Lucknow Coy Bde
	b		2	24		8	16			do

306 cylinders

Strength L.C.Bde Employed
Officers 4
⊗ Vide 46th Divn's G.791 of 10.8.16   NCOs 16
K.D.G.ds will supply this party   Men 222

Carrying Operations, Night of 13th/14th — Amendment to Appx A.

Rendezvous - BIENVILLERS. W.26.d.8.2.

Route in all parties. Dump → NAKED ST → turn right along support line and

No of Party	Officers	N.C.O.	O.R.	Time to report	Load	Emplacement	Route out	Unit Furnishing Party
				pm	Cylinders			
1	1	2	30	9.—	10	19	91 St → Left along fire trench	Neverending St → Lucknow Cav. B.
2 a	1	2	30	9.10	10	18		Ravine → Dump. "
2 b		2	30		10	17		"
3 a	1	2	24	9.20	8	1	90 St → Right along fire trench	8q St. and Stoneygate St. or Bienvillers Rd. "
3 b		2	30		10	2		"
4 a	1	2	30	9.30	10	3		"
4 b		2	24		8	4		"
5	1	2	24	9.40	8 / 4	5 / 6		"
6 a	1	2	30	9.50	10	8	91 St → Right along fire trench	"
6 b		2	24		8	9		"
7 a	1	2	30	10.—	10	14	"	137 Inf Bde
7 b		2	30		10	15		"
8	1	2	30	10.10	8	17	91 St → Left along F.T. Neverending St → Ravine	"
9 a	1	2	30	10.30	10	1	90 St → Right along fire trench	8q St. and Stoneygate Rd. or Bienvillers Road. "
9 b		2	30		10	2		"
10 a	1	2	30	10.40	10	3	91 St → right along fire trench	"
10 b		2	30		8 / 8	14 / 15		"
11	1	2	30	10.50	10	17	91 St → left along fire trench	Neverending St → Ravine → Dump "
12	1	2	30	11.10	10	1	90 St → right along F.T.	8q St → Stoneygate St "
13 a	1	2	30	11.30	10	17	91 St → Left along fire trench	Neverending St → Ravine → Dump. "
13 b		2	30		12	17		"

206 Cylinders

Carrying Operations. — Night of 13th/14th

Rendezvous BIENVILLERS. W.26.d.8.2.

No of Party	Officers	N.C.Os	O.R.	Time to Report	Load (cylinders)	Emplacement	Route in all parties → NAKED ST → turn right along support line	Route out	Unit Furnishing Party
1 {a	1	2	30	9 pm	10	20			137 Inf Bde
b		2	30		10	19	91 Street	NEVERENDING ST	"
2 {a	1	2	30	9.10	10	18	→ Left turn along	→ RAVINE → DUMP.	"
b		2	30		10	17	fire trench		
3 {a	1	2	24	9.20	8	1		→ 89 Street and	"
b		2	30		10	2	90 Street	STONEYGATE ST	"
4 {a	1	2	30	9.30	10	3	→ right turn along	(or BIENVILLERS RD)	"
b		2	24		8	4	fire trench		
5	1	2	30	9.40	10	8	→ 91 Street	→ 89 Street and	"
6 {a	1	2	30	9.50	10	15	→ turn right along	STONEYGATE ST	"
b		2	48		16	16	fire trench	(or BIENVILLERS RD)	"
7 {a	1	2	24	10.15	8	20	→ 91 Street	NEVERENDING ST	"
b		2	30		10	19	→ turn left along	→ RAVINE → DUMP	"
8		2	30	10.25	10	17	fire trench		"
9 {a	1	2	24	10.30	8	1	→ 90 Street	89 Street and	Buckn'm Co Rgt
b		2	30		10	2	→ right along	STONEYGATE RD	"
10	1	2	30	10.40	10	3	fire trench	(or BIENVILLERS RD)	
11	1	2	30	11.10	10	17	→ 91 Street → left along F.T.	NEVERENDING ST → RAVINE	"
12		2	24	11.10		7	→ 90 St → Right	89 St and STONEYGATE	"
13 {a	1	2	30	11.30	10	17	→ 91 St	NEVERENDING ST	"
b		2	30		10	17	→ Left along F.T.	→ RAVINE → DUMP	"

206 cylinders

11 Officers
41 NCOs
195 men

Amended vide appendix "A" for night 13/14 Aug issued with 46Dns 1878/1/G

B.M 486
2.11.8.16

S E C R E T.   46th Division.
                                                          1878/1/G.
  137th Inf. Bde.
  138th   do.
  139th   do.
  Lucknow Cav. Brigade.
  1/Monmouths.
  O.C. 'P' Coy. Special Bde. R.E.

        With reference to this Office 1878/G of 9th August, 1916,
Appendix 'A'. Owing to altered capacity of emplacements the
following amendments are made :-

Night of 11th/12th.

   Rendezvous - BERLES, W.21.b.65.15.

      Parties 4b)
           ,, 8b)   for emplacement 28 read 20.

        These deposit their load, turn about and go out by
NEVERENDING St.

   Rendezvous - BIENVILLERS, W.26.d.8.2.

      Party 1 a.   Load 10 cylinders   2 for emplacement 5.
                                             8   ,,   ,,   6.

      Party 7 a.   Load 10 cylinders.   8 ,,   ,,   4.
                                             2 ,,   ,,   5.

      Party 18.   Load 10 cylinders.   6 ,,   ,, 10.
                                             4 ,,   ,,   2.

        Strength of parties, times to report and routes remain
unaltered.

Night 12th/13th.

   Rendezvous - BERLES.

      Party 3.   For emplacement 29 read emplacement 26.

        ,, 4 b.   Load 10 cylinders.   2 for emplacement 32.
                                             8   ,,   ,,   32 A.

      Party 5 A.   Not required.

      Party 6.   for emplacement 32 read emplacement 32 A.

      Party 7 b.   Load 10 cylinders.   4 for emplacement 29.
                                             6   ,,   ,,   32 A.

   Rendezvous - BIENVILLERS.

      Parties 13 & 14.   Route in 91 St ⟶ turn left along fire-
trench.   Route out NEVERENDING St.
             All other routes remain unaltered.
      Party 11.   Load 12 cylinders.   8 for emplacement 10; 4 for
                                          emplacement 12.

                                                       Party

2.

    Party 13 a.   Load 10 cylinders.   2 for emplacement 18; 8 for emplacement 20.

    Party 16.   Load 12 cylinders.   8 for emplacement 10; 4 for emplacement 14.

Night 13th/14th.

    Rendezvous - BIENVILLERS.

    An amended page is issued herewith to Lucknow Cav. Bde., 137th Inf. Brigade; 138th Inf. Brigade (for Traffic Officers) and 'P' Coy. Special Bde. R.E.

11th August, 1916.   *I.D Gutting* Capt.   Lieut-Col.,
                                                  General Staff, 46th Division.

SERIAL No. 111

Confidential

War Diary

of

Headquarters, Lucknow Cavalry Brigade

FROM 1st September 1916 TO 30th September 1916

Army Form C. 2118.

Lucknow Bde H.Q.

LUCKNOW CAVALRY BRIGADE.

WAR DIARY

or

INTELLIGENCE SUMMARY

(Erase heading not required.)

Instructions regarding War Diaries and Intelligence Summaries are contained in F. S. Regs., Part II, and the Staff Manual respectively. Title pages will be prepared in manuscript.

Hour, Date, Place.	Summary of Events and Information.	Remarks and references to Appendices
September 1st PAS.		
do. 3rd do.	The working parties K.D.Gds and 29th Lancers were relieved by Infantry and rejoined their units. G.O.C. VII Corps expressed his appreciation of the willing services rendered by the Brigade. The Brigade marched via HAUTE VISÉE to billets at OCCOCHES (B.H.Q. & M.G.S.) – OUTRE-BOIS (29th Lrs) – MEZEROLLES (K.D.G) – BARLY (36th J.H.), and rejoined 1st Indian Cavalry Division.	
do. 4th OCCOCHES.	Marched to billets near ST. RIQUIER for training – units billeted as follows (B.H.Q. & M.G.S.) - BRAILLY – K.D.G., CANCHY – 36th J.H., GAPENNES – 29th Lrs., DOMVAST.	
do. 11th BRAILLY.	Brigade returned to billeting area at FROHEN (B.H.Q., K.D.G., M.G.S.) – (36th J.H.) – BEAUVOIR RIVIERE – (29th Lrs) BEALCOURT.	
do. 12th do.	Marched to billets at HEM (B.H.Q. & 36th J.H.)–GROUCHES (K.D.G., & 29000000 M.G.S.) – BOUT des PRES (29th Lrs).	Appendix 1
do. 13th do.	Marched as a Division to bivouac at area "W" north of QUERRIEU. Brigade Hd Qrs to ALLONVILLE.	March Table attached Appendix 2
do. 15th do.	Marched at 5.0 a.m. in accordance with Divisional Operation Order No. 26 to Preliminary Position South of DERNACOURT and remained at 1 hours notice to move. "A" Echelon marched ... Divisionalized under O.C., A.S.G. to Preliminary Position. "B" Echelon remained in bivouac at QUERRIEU.	3
do. 15th DERNACOURT.	Brigade remained at 1 hours notice to move during the day, at night this was relaxed.	4
do. 17th	1 1st, 3rd British Divisions & 2nd I.C.D returned to QUERRIEU – 2nd British & 1st I.C.D remained at 1 hour	

LUCKNOW CAVALRY BRIGADE.

WAR DIARY or INTELLIGENCE SUMMARY.

(Erase heading not required.)

Army Form C. 2118.

Instructions regarding War Diaries and Intelligence Summaries are contained in F. S. Regs., Part II, and the Staff Manual respectively. Title pages will be prepared in manuscript.

Hour, Date, Place.	Summary of Events and Information.	Remarks and references to Appendices
September 20th DERNACOURT.	Brigade put on 3 hours notice to move from time of receipt of orders. B.H.Q. moved Camp up to high ground N.E. of MORLANCOURT. During this period officers patrols reconnoitred the Cavalry tracks up to the front line which had been made by the dismounted men of the Cavalry Corps, which had been reformed.	
do. 25th MORLANCOURT.	In accordance with Brigade Operation Order attached, the Brigade remained at 1 hour's notice to move from "Zero" hour (12.35 p.m.)	Appendix ⑤
do. 25th do. 7.34 p.m.	Orders received that Brigade would not be moved up and that remainder of Division was returning to bivouac at MORLANCOURT that night.	⑥
do. 26th MORLANCOURT.	Orders received that Brigade would be prepared to march back to G.H.Q. area at 3.0 p.m.	⑦
do. do. 12.45 p.m.	Telephone orders received for Brigade to saddle up at once and be ready to move to MAMETZ.	⑨
do. do. 12.50 p.m.	K.D.Gds ordered to proceed at once to MAMETZ and to send an officers group to liaise with 21st Division at MONTAUBAN. O.C., K.D.Gds to report arrival to Cavalry Corps through 21st Division.	

LUCKNOW CAVALRY BRIGADE.

WAR DIARY or INTELLIGENCE SUMMARY.

(Erase heading not required.)

Army Form C. 2118.

Instructions regarding War Diaries and Intelligence Summaries are contained in F.S. Regs., Part II, and the Staff Manual respectively. Title page will be prepared in manuscript.

Hour, Date, Place.	Summary of Events and Information.	Remarks and references to Appendices
September 26th MORLANCOURT. 1.20 p.m.	K.D.Gds moved off to MAMETZ and Brigade remained saddled up. "U" Battery R.H.A., and Lucknow Field Ambulance were attached to Brigade and 1 troop Field Squadron ordered to join Brigade on arrival at MAMETZ. O.C. Signal Troop and Brigade Intelligence Officer (Capt. S.E.HARVEY, K.D.G) were sent on with K.D.Gds. The regiment arrived at MAMETZ at 2.0 p.m. and O.C. proceeded to 21st Division who had no orders for him. Later he received orders to take the regiment to WATERLOT Fm. and to send an officers patrol to gain touch with the Squadron 19th Lrs., and another to reconnoitre the route to GUEDECOURT.	Appendix ⑨
do. do. 3.50 p.m.	Remainder of Brigade ordered to move at once by phone to Cavalry Corps. G.O.C., C.O's and B.M. proceeded at once in car to MONTAUBAN to find out situation from G.O.C. 21st Division, and Brigade marched at once, with "A" echelon, by Cavalry track to MAMETZ reaching there 6.0 p.m.	⑩
do. do. 5.15 p.m.	G.O.C. and C.O's arrived at MONTAUBAN and found that 21st Division had no instructions regarding them and that the opportunity for cavalry action had apparently passed. K.D.Gds were then in signal communication from WATERLOT Fm. and O.C. was ordered to send in situation report. His liaison officer reported that patrols were out towards GUEDECOURT but so far no information had been received. No orders had yet been received by G.O.C. as to plan of action.	

Army Form C. 2118.

LUCKNOW CAVALRY BRIGADE.

WAR DIARY

or

INTELLIGENCE SUMMARY.

(Erase heading not required.)

Instructions regarding War Diaries and Intelligence Summaries are contained in F. S. Regs., Part II, and the Staff Manual respectively. Title pages will be prepared in manuscript.

Hour, Date, Place.	Summary of Events and Information.	Remarks and references to Appendices
September 26th MONTAUBAN. 6.30 p.m.	Permission was given by Corps to withdraw K.D.Gds to bivouac at MONTAUBAN and orders were sent to rear report centre to tell Brigade to bivouac at MAMETZ and be saddled up at 6.0 a.m. and ready to move. Advanced report centre remained in MONTAUBAN. Meanwhile officers patrols K.D.Gds reported that they had reconnoitred the route to GUEDECOURT and had gained touch with the Squadron 19th Lrs., which was returning to MAMETZ. The patrols had a few casualties from shrapnel.	Appendix (11)
do. 7.30 p.m.	O.C., 19th Lrs Squadron reported that he had been in action with enemy East of GUEDECOURT and had been relieved by infantry. This report was phoned to Corps.	
do. 9.0 p.m.	As no further orders were received G.O.C. issued attached orders to O.C., K.D.Gds detailing two Squadrons to proceed at 6.0 a.m. to position of readiness at WATERLOT Fm. and to send two officers patrols No.1 to reconnoitre route S. of DELVILLE Wood and S. of GUEDECOURT for Cavalry advance - to gain touch with infantry and report any suitable opportunity for cavalry action. No. had similar duties moving E. of FLERS towards LIGNY THILLOY. Reports were to be sent in to MONTAUBAN from the nearest Brigade advanced report centre. Remainder of Brigade to be ready to move at 1 hours notice.	Appendix (12)

Army Form C. 2118.

LUCKNOW CAVALRY BRIGADE.

WAR DIARY
or
INTELLIGENCE SUMMARY.
(Erase heading not required.)

Instructions regarding War Diaries and Intelligence Summaries are contained in F. S. Regs., Part II, and the Staff Manual respectively. Title page will be prepared in manuscript.

Hour, Date, Place.	Summary of Events and Information.	Remarks and references to Appendices
September 26th MONTAUBAN. 10.30 p.m.	Brigade recieved orders to move back on the following morning to previous bivouac and thence to BUSSY les DAOURS. Previous orders were cancelled and orders issued for Brigade to march at 8.0 a.m. to MORLANCOURT - water and feed there and thence to BUSSY.	Appendix 13
September 27th MONTAUBAN. 8.0 a.m.	Brigade moved off to MORLANCOURT and reached there 11.0 a.m. moved on again at 3.0 p.m. and reached bivouac at BUSSY 6.0 p.m.	
September 28th BUSSY les DAOURS 8.30 a.m.	Brigade marched via AMIENS and road S. of SOMME to billets as follows. B.H.Q., K.D.Gds. 29th Lrs.; M.G.S., HANGEST "U" Battery and 36th J.H. CROUY.	
September 29th HANGEST. 8.0 a.m.	Brigade marched at 8.0 a.m. via CONDE - L'ETOILE - COCQUEREL to billets as follows. B.H.Q.; BOIS de L'ABBEY - "U" Batty and M.G.S. BEAUCOURT - K.D.Gds YAUCHELLES - 29th Lrs BELLANCOURT 36th J.H. PONT REMY - M.V.S. MONTFLIERS.	
September 30th BOIS de L'ABBEY. 8.0 a.m.	Brigade marched at 8.0 a.m. via ABBEVILLE - HAUTVILLERS - FOREST L'ABBEY - CRECY - to billets, B.H.Q.; 36th J.H.; M.G.S., CRECY - "U" Batty ROSSIGNIL - K.D.Gds MACHY - 29th Lrs., MACHIEL M.V.S., Saw Mills 1 mile W. of CRECY.	

Major,
Brigade Major, Lucknow Cavalry Brigade.

SECRET.   Copy No. 10

Lucknow Cavalry Brigade Operation Order No. 1.

Dated 12th September, 1916.

Reference 1/100,000 Sheets LENS and AMIENS.

The Division will march on the 13th instant to a billeting area North of QUERRIEU.

The Divisional Starting Point will be the road Junction about 550 yards South West of the S in STA of BEAUVAL, Divisional Troops Starting Point-Road Junction North East of CITADELLE-DOULLENS.

"B" Echelon will be divisionalised and march under order of O.C., A.S.C.

2.   Reference above the Brigade (less "B" Echelon) will rendezvous head on the HULEUX-BEAUVAL — DOULLENS-BEAUVAL road fork at 2.30 p.m.

Order of March.—
Signal Troop.
36th J. Horse.
29th Lancers.
K. D. Gds.
M. G. Sqdn.   (detailed by O.C., 29
"A" Echelon in order of units (under an officer

The route to billets will be TALMAS — VILLERS-BOCAGE — MOLLIENS-au-BOIS — ST. GRATIEN — no other roads to be used.

At cross roads N.W. of TALMAS the column will pass "B" Echelon at a trot and walk. Head of the Brigade is to reach this point at 4.15 p.m.

Units will move to Brigade Starting Point by DOULLENS — AMIENS road. 36th J. Horse will use the road passing N. of the CITADELLE DOULLENS.

                              under B.T.O.

3.   "B" Echelon, (under an Officer to be detailed by O.C., K. D. Gds) and M.V.S. will rendezvous in order of Units at X roads Le BONAIR at 1.30 p.m. and will pass Divisional Starting Point at 2.30 p.m.

Routes to Starting Point and thence to billets as for fighting troops.

The cyclists of the Brigade will march Brigaded in rear of "A" Echelon under a senior N.C.O. to be detailed by O.C., K. D. Gds.

4.   Report Centre will close at HEM and open at ALLONVILLE at 12 noon.

                                              Major,
                    Brigade Major, Lucknow Cavalry Brigade.

Issued at 11.30 a.m.

        Copies No. 1 - 10 as per Brigade Standing Orders.
              No. 11   1st Indian Cavalry Division.

(2)

MARCH TABLE TO ACCOMPANY 1ST INDIAN CAVALRY DIVISION OPERATION ORDER NO.26.

Unit.	To be clear of R.L'HALLUE.	Instructions.	To be clear of main ALBERT Rd.	To reach BONNAY Bridge.	To be clear of Riy.Bridge S.E. of BONNAY.	Remarks.
MHOW Bde (less "A" Echelon Wheeled).	5.0.a.m.	Not to cross ALBERT Road till 5.45.a.m.	6.0.a.m.	7.15.a.m.	8.0.a.m.	(a) Each Bde will use all crossings over River L'HALLUE in turn.
LUCKNOW Bde (less "A" Echelon Wheeled).	6.0.a.m.		7.0.a.m.	8.0.a.m.	8.45.a.m.	(b) Brigades will form up in mass North of main ALBERT - QUERRIEU road in the place shown to Bde Majors. Will cross that road in mass and will proceed across country between B.MaCaine and B.ESCAPLONNEUSE, and join the LA HAUSSUE - BONNAY road at the 4 large trees near road junction East of ESCARDONNEUSE, through BONNAY to track leading through T of AERICOURT L'ABBE.
SIALKOT Bde (less "A" Echelon wheeled). (c)	7.0.a.m.		8.0.a.m.	9.0.a.m.	9.45.a.m.	
JODHPUR LANCERS (less "A" Echelon wheeled).	7.30.a.m.		8.15.a.m.	9.30.a.m.	10.15.a.m. and to arrive at bivouacs by 12 noon.	(c) SIALKOT Bde will get all horses at present West of L'HALLUE River clear of the passage between bridges

MARCH TABLE (continued).

Unit.	Starting Point.	Time to pass Starting Point.	Route.	Remarks.
Commander.- Lt.Col.CHARLTON, R.H.A.				
(d). DIVL.HDQRS. SIGNAL SCDN. R.H.A.BDE. FIELD SQN.	Junction of ALLON-VILLE - QUERRIEU and ST GRATIEN - QUERRIEU roads.	5.0.a.m.	QUERRIEU PONTNOYELLES, LA NEUVILLE, CORBIE, FRAY road as far as track leading through T of MERICOURT -L'ABBE to bivouacs.	Intervals will be left between points passing through LA NEUVILLE and CORBIE as far as track mentioned in column 4 to allow passage of other troops in Sector.
(ii) Commander- O.C.A.S.C. Divl.H.Q. Wheeled "A" Echelon.				
MHOW BDE ---do---				
LUCKNOW BDE ---do---				
SIALKOT BDI. ---do---				
JODHPUR LAICERS ---do---				
DIVL.AMMN.COL:(less G.S. Wagons).				
AMBULANCES (less G.S. Wagons).		to be clear of QUERRIEU by 6.15.a.m.		
LIMBERED TRAIN Wagons).				

"A" Form.
MESSAGES AND SIGNALS.

Army Form C. 2121.

Prefix	Code	m.	Words	Charge	This message is on a/c of:	Recd. at	m.
Office of Origin and Service Instructions.			Sent At ___ m. To ___ By ___		_____ Service. (Signature of "Franking Officer.")	Date From By	

TO { Sialkot Bde.   Jodhpur Lancers. A.D.V.S.   "Q"
     Mhow   "   Field Sqdn.   O.C.K.S.C. A.P.M.
     Lucknow "   Signal   "   Intern. Off. 4th Army
     R.H.A. "   A.D.M.S.   Camp Commdt. Cav. Corps

Sender's Number	Day of Month	In reply to Number	AAA
C.A.368.	16/9/		

Operation Order No.29. AAA No further information beyond that already issued AAA Units will bivouac in the positions occupied last night AAA 1st Ind.Cav.Divn. will be ready to move within one hour of receiving orders from 10.0.a.m. 17th inst.

From: 1st Ind. Cav. Divn.
Place:
Time: 7.30.p.m.

Major,

"A" Form. Army Form C. 2121.

MESSAGES AND SIGNALS.

Secret

TO: Sialkot Bde., Mhow, Lucknow, Jodhpur Lancers, Field Sqdn., Signal, O.C. A.S.C., A.D.V.S., Camp Comdt., A.P.M., Interp. Off.

Sender's Number: C.A.370. Day of Month: 17/9/ AAA

2nd British Cavalry Division and 1st Indian Cavy. Divn. remain in present areas but must be ready to move at one hours notice AAA The other three Cav. Divns. are returning to their areas round QUERRIEU AAA Brigades will continue to reconnoitre the forward approaches as far as they are permitted.

BM.39
GA 370.

From: 1st Ind. Cav. Divn.
Place:
Time:

G.S.

SECRET.
B.M. 110

Headquarters,
Lucknow Cavalry Brigade.
25th September, 1916.

To, O.C., K.D.Gds   M.G.S.   O.C., "A" Echelon.
     29th Lrs.   Sig Troop.   Sialkot M.V.S.
     36th J.H.   A.D.C.

1.   If the Brigade is ordered to move up to MAMETZ the route followed will be that shewn to guides yesterday.

        Order of March.-
            Signal Troop.
            K.D.Gds.
            29th Lrs.
            36th J.H.
            M.G.S.
            "A" Echelon in order of units (under Lt. HATFIELD
                                                    K.D.Gs).
            Sialkot M.V.S.

      Brigade Starting Point will be the junction of the track and the MORLANCOURT - MEAULTE road, Head of Brigade to pass that point 1 hour after receipt of orders.

2.   In the event of Brigade not having moved by 6.30 p.m. the officer responsible for lighting the track will take out their lamp parties and post them along the sections for which they are responsible. A guard of a N.C.O. and 6 men per Regiment will bivouac in central place in each sector and will be responsible for keeping the lamps alight and that they are collected and brought on when Sialkot M.V.S. have passed. If no move takes place they will return to Camp at dawn -- after posting their parties the officers will return and be ready to guide their Regiments.

3.   O.C., K.D.Gds will detail a trumpeter to be on duty at B.H.Q., from 2.0 p.m. today.

                                            Major,
                            Brigade Major, Lucknow Cavalry Brigade.

※ These officers will report at B.H.Q. on their way out.

"A" Form.
MESSAGES AND SIGNALS.
Army Form C.2121 (in pads of 100).

Prefix	Code	m.	Words	Charge	This message is on a/c of:	Recd. at .... m.
			Sent		..................Service.	Date...... ⑥
Office of Origin and Service Instructions.			At......m. To By		(Signature of "Franking Officer.")	From By

TO: Sialkot / Mhow / 5 / 7 RHA Bde / F Sigs Sqdn Cav Corps / N Midd 18/S 1st Indian / N BdC / Capt Smith RFC Sqdn RFC / RFC Liaison Off

Sender's Number: GA407   Day of Month: 25-9-16   In reply to Number: 15 Corps / 21 Divn

AAA

The Own Less LUCKNOW Bde will return to bivouac at MORLANCOURT using the same route as this morning aaa SIALKOT Bde will lead followed by Divisional Troops less ambulances followed by MHOW Bde aaa Major PAYNTER will command Divl Troops which will march in the same order as this morning aaa SIALKOT Bde will leave one squadron at MAMETZ which will come in duty at FRICOURT at 7am under the same conditions as before and report by telephone to Cav Corps (advd) aaa LUCKNOW Bde will be duty Brigade tomorrow 26th inst and be ready to move at one hours notice from day aaa The Field squadron will concentrate in its original bivouac aaa 7 Fld ambs will follow behind MHOW Bde Report centre will be at

From MONTAUBAN at 7.30pm and open at FRICOURT at same time aa will close at FRICOURT at 9pm and open Place at MORLANCOURT at same time aaa
Time

The above may be forwarded as now corrected.   (Z)

From 2nd Ind Cav Divn   7.34pm   Censor.   Signature of Addressor or person authorised to telegraph in his name.

"A" Form.   Army Form C. 2121.
MESSAGES AND SIGNALS.   No. of Message ....

Prefix ...... Code ...... m	Words	Charge	This message is on a/c of:	Recd. at ...... m
Office of Origin and Service Instructions.	Sent		Service.	Date
To be 6.20am	At ...... m			From
	To			By
	By		(Signature of "Franking Officer.")	

TO | THREE Bde · R.A.A. Bde · Fd Sqdn
   | Signal Sqdn · Camp Commdt
   | OC ABC · ADVS ADMS DADOS APM

| Sender's Number | Day of Month | In reply to Number | | AAA |
| GA 408 | 26-9 | | | |

Division will be prepared to move this afternoon aaa No details received

From   1st Ind Cav Div
Place
Time   6.0 am
                        (Z) G.R.Rankard
                        Censor.   Signature of Addressor or person authorised to telegraph in his name.
                                    for G.S.

"A" Form.
MESSAGES AND SIGNALS.

Army Form C. 2121.

TO	Lucknow	ADMS	Fd Sqdn	21st Div
	2/Lancs Bde	ADVS	O.C ASC	Cav Corps
	A/mm	1st and RHA Bde	Signals	

Sender's Number: GA 411
Day of Month: 26/9

AAA

Lucknow Bde will saddle up at once AAA Directly K.D.G have saddled up they will send one Sqdn at once to MAMETZ and despatch an Officers group to get into touch with 21st Division at MONTAUBAN AAA Remainder of Division will be at one hours notice.

BM 118

From: 1st Ind Cav Div.
Time: 12.50 AM

"A" Form.
MESSAGES AND SIGNALS.

Army Form C.2121 (in pads of 100).
No. of Message ....

Prefix ...... Code ...... m.	Words	Charge	This message is on a/c of:	Recd. at .... m.
Office of Origin and Service Instructions.	Sent			Date ....
....	At .... m.		.... Service.	From (9a)
....	To			By ....
....	By		(Signature of "Franking Officer.")	

TO { *H. 6. K. ee 36 F.*
— 9th Div — M.S.R.

Sender's Number.	Day of Month.	In reply to Number.	A A A
* Bm 32.	26.7.16.		

1. If Brigade is ordered to move ord
order of march will be :—

   89th
   36th
   M.S.
   11 Battery.
   A Broken under to H.field RHA
   M.T.S.
   Mon ko Arti. L.C.F.A

2. Brigade starting point will be
Brigade Head Quarters Camp
After leaving camp Bde report centre
will be at Head of 89th Division

3. If no further words are received Bde will decide in
above order, is BUSSY. Starting point & track at B52.6.

From			
Place			
Time			

The above may be forwarded as now corrected. (Z) *Arm Turner Major*

Censor. Signature of Addressor or person authorised to telegraph in his name.

Oh. L. C. Bde

* This line should be erased if not required.

"A" Form.
MESSAGES AND SIGNALS.

Army Form C. 2121.

TO	Sialkot	Ya Sqdn	A.D.V.S.	O.C.A.S.C.
	Lucknow	Signals	&	Camp Comdt
	R.H.A. Bde	A.D.M.S.	MHow Bde	

Sender's Number: G.A. 414
Day of Month: 26/9/-

Remaining Regts of LUCKNOW Bde with "U" Bty R.H.A. will move up immediately to south of MAMETZ AAA. They will report hour of departure to Div HdQrs and their arrival at above position to Cav Corps AAA SIALKOT Bde will stand by ready to move up on receipt of orders to that effect AAA Q Bty R.H.A. and a portion of Fd Amblces will accompany SIALKOT Bde AAA MHOW Bde will also stand fast at present and return to bivouac ready to move AAA Div. Troops will not move till further orders.

From: 1st Ind Cav D.

Lt Col
G.S.

MESSAGES AND SIGNALS.

Army Form C. 2121.

TO: B.M. Lucknow Bde.

Sender's Number.	Day of Month	In reply to Number	
1	26	BM.130	AAA

Orders received from Cav. Corps. AAA To bring the Regt. to S 23. d. and to send patrol to GUEDECOURT to try and find the 19th Lancers. AAA One patrol to GUEDECOURT to reconnoitre the road there AAA. Am to report to Cav. Corps as soon as patrol comes in. AAA. Regt. Report centre near WATERLOT FARM in a dug out about S.24.a.2-8

rec'd 6.30 pm

From: K.D.G.
Place:
Time: 6.15 pm

"A" Form. Army Form C. 2121.
MESSAGES AND SIGNALS. No. of Message_____

Prefix... Code...m. Office of Origin and Service Instructions.	Words	Charge	This message is on a/c of: ....Service. (Signature of "Franking Officer.")	Recd. at.........m. Date......(11)...... From............ By
	Sent At.........m. To............ By			

| TO | H. Battery KDG 2nd | 36th MGS MGS | Field Troop "Ambulance Cav Corps | 1st I.C.D |

Sender's Number	Day of Month	In reply to Number	
BM 133	26		AAA

Bde will off saddle & go into bivouac AAA KDG will withdraw to MONTAUBAN by any track and send an officer now to report to Advd Bde report Centre AAA They will bivouac in MONTAUBAN or MAMETZ AAA Regts to be at 1 hours notice from 7.0 am tomorrow. AAA KDG are to keep in touch with situation towards GUEDECOURT by means of patrols AAA Patrols to report via Advd 64th Bde to Advd Bde report centre AAA Report centre remaining with 21st Div MONTAUBAN

From B. M.
Place
Time

Signature of Addressee or person authorised to telegraph in his name.

"A" Form. Army Form C. 2121.

MESSAGES AND SIGNALS. No. of Message_____

TO: O.C. K.D.G.
Cav. Corps.

Sender's Number: BM 134
Day of Month: 26
AAA

1. The mission of Lucknow Cav. Bde is to keep touch with the infantry towards GUEUDECOURT with view to making use of any opportunity which may arise of pushing patrols E & N of that village to report whether situation is favourable for Cavalry action.

2. With this object two Squadrons K.D.G.s will march at 6.0am tomorrow to a position of readiness about S.23.d. These Squadrons will send out two patrols, as follows:—

No. 1. Patrol to reconnoitre a suitable route in continuation of Cavalry track running S.E. of DELVILLE wood along which mounted troops can advance E of GUEDECOURT towards high ground E of that village. If situation permits that this patrol can pass E of GUEUDECOURT,

"A" Form. Army Form C. 2121.
MESSAGES AND SIGNALS. No. of Message_____

Prefix....Code....m.	Words	Charge	This message is on a/c of:	Recd. at...........m.
Office of Origin and Service Instructions.				Date..................
	Sent		...................Service.	
	At.............m.			From..................
	To			
	By		(Signature of "Franking Officer.")	By....................

TO

Sender's Number	Day of Month	In reply to Number	
			AAA

2 Coy — it will reconnoitre towards BEAULENCOURT.

No 2. Patrol will reconnoitre suitable route towards LIGNY THILLOY passing E of FLERS. This patrol will similarly be guided by situation of our infantry W of GUEUDECOURT before advancing on LIGNY THILLOY.

These patrols will first gain touch with 64th Bde Advd Report Centre at N 32 c central, whence No 2 Patrol will enquire for the nearest infantry Bde Advd Report centre of the Brigade on the left, & will gain touch with infantry W of GUEUDECOURT by that means. Reports from these patrols to be transmitted if possible every hour through infantry Bde report centres direct to LUCKNOW advd report centre via MONTAUBAN exchange.

From
Place
Time

The above may be forwarded as now corrected. (Z)

Censor._____ Signature of Addressee or person authorised to telegraph in his name.

* This line should be erased if not required.
T. & W. & J. M. Ltd., London. W 14042/M44. 75,000 12/15. Forms C 2121/10.

"A" Form.   Army Form C. 2121.

MESSAGES AND SIGNALS. No. of Message_____

Prefix......Code......m.	Words	Charge	This message is on a/c of:	Recd. at........m.
Office of Origin and Service Instructions.	Sent			Date..............
....	At.........m.		..................Service.	From.............
....	To............			
....	By............		(Signature of "Franking Officer.")	By...............

| TO { | | III | | |

Sender's Number	Day of Month	In reply to Number		
*	26.			A A A

3. Remainder of Brigade will remain in present bivouac ready to move at 1 hours notice.

From   B.M.
Place   MONTAUBAN
Time   9.20 pm.

The above may be forwarded as now corrected.   (Z)   A.M.Turner Maj.

.... Censor.   Signature of Addressor or person authorised to telegraph in his name.

* This line should be erased if not required.

SECRET.   Copy No........ 13

1st Indian Cavalry Division Operation Order No.34.
Dated September 27th 1916.

Reference ALBERT Combined Sheet 1/40,000 & 1/100,000 Sheet 17.

1. 1st Indian Cavalry Division Operation Order No.33 is cancelled.

2. 1st Indian Cavalry Division will move to bivouacs about BUSSY-LES-DAOURS this afternoon.

3. Brigades will march with their batteries and "A" Echelon wheels passing the Divisional Starting Point at the times given below.

    They will move by the track they came, BONNAY, DAOURS to BUSSY-LES-DAOURS.

4. Divisional Troops will be under command of Lieut-Colonel HOLDEN, 5th Cavalry, and will march via the track mentioned above, CORBIE, LA NEUVILLE, DAOURS to BUSSY-LES-DAOURS.

5. Divisional Starting Point will be the cross tracks in K.1.b. 6½.6.

6. Times to pass Divisional Starting Point and order of march will be :-

    MHOW Brigade..........12 noon.
    SIALKOT Brigade........1.p.m.
    DIVL. TROOPS.

    DIVL. H.Qrs.   )
    SIGNAL SQDN.   )
    R.H.A. BDE. H.QRS.   )
    JODHPUR LANCERS.   )
    DIVL. AMMN. COLUMN   ) 2.p.m.
        (less 1 Section).   )
    "A" ECHELON of the above.)
    FIELD AMBLCES (less   )
        1 Ambulance).   )

    LUCKNOW Brigade.   )
    FIELD SQUADRON.   ) 3.p.m.
    1 SECTION DIVL.AMMN.COLUMN.)
    LUCKNOW CAVY.FD.AMBLCE.   )

7. FIELD SQUADRON will march with the LUCKNOW BRIGADE.

8. The Division will move to an area further West on the 28th.

9. Report Centre will close at MORLANCOURT at 3.p.m. and open at BUSSY-LES-DAOURS at the same hour.

                                        C.A.C. Godwin.
                                        Lieut-Colonel,
                                        G.S. 1st Indian Cavalry Division.

Issued to Signals at 6.30.a.m.

        Copy No. 1. Sialkot Bde.   Copy No.12. French Inter.
         "   " 2. Mhow   "   "   " 13. Camp Comdt.
         "   " 3. Lucknow "   "   " 14. A.P.M.
         "   " 4. R.H.A. Bde.   "   " 15. R.F.C. Liaison
         "   " 5. Field Sqdn.   "   " 16. Cavalry Corp
         "   " 6. Signal Sqdn.   "   " 17. Col. RICHIE,
         "   " 7. Jodhpur Lancers.   18th Sqdn. R.
         "   " 8. A.D.M.S.   "   " 18. XV Corps.
         "   " 9. A.D.V.S.   "   " 19. 21st Divn.
         "   " 10-11 "Q"   "   " 20. Fourth Army
                                             "   " 21-24, File, Offi
               35. O.C.A.S.C.   & Diary.

SERIAL NO. 111.

Confidential
War Diary
of

Headquarters, Lucknow Cavalry Brigade.

FROM 1st October 1916 TO 31st October 30th November 1916.

Army Form C. 2118.

LUCKNOW CAVALRY BRIGADE.
WAR DIARY
or
INTELLIGENCE SUMMARY
(Erase heading not required.)

OCTOBER 1916.

Instructions regarding War Diaries and Intelligence Summaries are contained in F. S. Regs., Part II. and the Staff Manual respectively. Title Pages will be prepared in manuscript.

Place	Date	Hour	Summary of Events and Information	Remarks and references to Appendices
CRECY.	1st	—	NO CHANGE.	
"	19th.	9-45 a.m.	"U" Battery, R.H.A. marched with 1st Indian R.H.A. Brigade to NOEUX for attachment to 1st Cavalry Division for ensuing operations.	
"	22nd.	8-15 a.m.	The Machine Gun Squadron, strength 5 B.O's, 4 I.O's, 78 B.O.R., 118 I.O.R. and 37 animals under Captain A.A.Mercer left for attachment to Reserve Army.	
"	22nd	4,30 p.m.	"U" Battery, R.H.A. rejoined Brigade owing to the Ammunition Column having several cases of pink eye.	
"	31st	—	NO CHANGE.	

Major,
for G.O.C., Lucknow Cavalry Brigade.

Army Form C. 2118.

WAR DIARY
of
INTELLIGENCE SUMMARY.
(Erase heading not required.)

LUCKNOW CAVALRY BRIGADE

Instructions regarding War Diaries and Intelligence Summaries are contained in F. S. Regs., Part II, and the Staff Manual respectively. Title pages will be prepared in manuscript.

Hour, Date, Place.	Summary of Events and Information.	Remarks and references to Appendices.
1-11-16 CRECY.	No change.	
2-11-16 "	Brigade marched in 3 columns to a new billeting area as follows:- B.H.Q., 'U' Battery R.H.A., Section Ammn Column MOYENNEVILLE, K.D.Gds, MIANNAY, BOUILLANCOURT, and LAMBERCOURT. 36th J.Horse, QUESNOY LE-MONTANT and CAHON. 29th Lancers, CHEPY and ACHEUX. Mobile Vety Section, HYMMEVILLE.	
17-11-16 MOYENNEVILLE.	Indian personnel with Signal Troop returned to Units, and replaced by British ranks from Base.	
19-11-16 "	'U' Battery R.H.A. and Section Ammunition Column left for attachment to Fourth Army School.	
20-11-16 "	Jodhpur Lancers attached to Brigade for training and administration.	
21-11-16 "	A Pioneer Battalion, strength 31 officers 827 other ranks left Brigade for work under 1st Anzac Corps. The Battalion entrained at PONT REMY, detrained at MERICOURT, and went into camp near FRICOURT (F 8.C.5.5,Sheet 62 D, 1/40,000). The two Indian Companies were employed on the LONGUEVAL-FLERS railway; the British Company on water lines in MAMETZ Valley.	
27-11-16 "	The Lucknow M.G.Squadron rejoined Brigade from 31st Divn and were billeted in HYMMEVILLE, QUESNOY, FRIERES.	

Major.
Brigade Major, Lucknow Cavalry Brigade.

SERIAL No. 111

Confidential
War Diary
of

Headquarters, Lucknow Cavalry Brigade.

FROM 1st December 1916 TO 31st December 1916.

No. 1

WAR DIARY.

OF

LUCKNOW CAVALRY BRIGADE HEADQUARTERS.

For the month of

DECEMBER, 1916.

Army Form C. 2118.

WAR DIARY
or
INTELLIGENCE SUMMARY.

LUCKNOW CAVALRY BRIGADE.
(Erase heading not required.)

Instructions regarding War Diaries and Intelligence Summaries are contained in F. S. Regs., Part II, and the Staff Manual respectively. Title pages will be prepared in manuscript.

Hour, Date, Place.		Summary of Events and Information.	Remarks and references to Appendices.
MOYENNEVILLE.			
1st to 13th December		NO CHANGE.	
14th December,	10.0 a.m.	Transport Relief of Pioneer Btn., strength 6 L.G.S and 4 G.S.W. left Bde. Hdqrs. rationed up to the 16th.	
14th do.	2.0 a.m.	Departure of Relief Party for Pioneer Btn., strength 17 Offrs. 353 O.R.	
14th do.	2.15 p.m.	Arrival at Railhead of Relieved Party, strength 19 Offrs. 356 O.R. who were distributed to their units in lorries.	
14th do.	-	M.V.Section took over billets at CHAUSSOY-LES-TROUFLES vacated by the Detachment A.H.T. Coy.	
15th do.	-	NO CHANGE.	
16th do.	-	Relieved transport of Pioneer Btn., rejoined units 18th inst. having being handed over to 2/Lieut. A.BROWN, K.D.Gs. 9.0 a.m. 16th at LE CARCAILLOT.	
17th do.	-	NO CHANGE.	
18th do.	-	29th Lancers Section M.G.S. moved into FRIREULLES.	
19th do.	-	Section Jod.Cav.Fld.Amb. vacated MONCHAUX and went into billets at FRANLEU. 1 Squadron Jodhpur Lrs. moved into FRANLEU from FRIREULLES.	
20th to 31st December		NO CHANGE.	

S.E. Hawey Captain,
for Brigade Major, Lucknow Cavalry Brigade.

www.ingramcontent.com/pod-product-compliance
Lightning Source LLC
Chambersburg PA
CBHW080854230426
43662CB00013B/2102